Boundaries, Walls and Fences

Boundaries, Walls and Fences

Eighth Edition

Trevor M Aldridge
QC (Hon), MA (Cantab), Solicitor

LAW & TAX

© Pearson Professional Limited 1997

ISBN 0752 004131

Eighth Edition 1997

Published by
FT Law & Tax
21–27 Lamb's Conduit Street
London WC1N 3NJ

A Division of Pearson Professional Limited

Associated Offices
Australia, Belgium, Canada, Hong Kong, India, Japan, Luxembourg,
Singapore, Spain, USA

First Published 1962

A CIP catalogue record for this book is available from the British
Library

Printed and bound in Great Britain by Biddles

Contents

Table of Cases

Table of Statutes

Table of Statutory Instruments

Introduction

'Boundaries are notorious troublemakers'
Lloyd v *Stanbury* [1971] 1 WLR 535, 542 per Brightman J

'O wall, O sweet, O lovely wall,
That standest between her father's ground and mine'
Midsummer Night's Dream, William Shakespeare

'Good fences make good neighbours'
North of Boston. Mending Wall, Robert Frost

The law relating to party walls has been radically altered by the Party Wall etc Act 1996. For a long time there has been local legislation relating only to inner London. The new Act extends this, in amended form, to the whole country. Property owners will now have rights to insist upon making alterations to party walls so that they fit in with their development proposals, and to build on boundaries where there is no division wall. Their neighbours have rights to challenge the proposals, to require them to be adapted and to have compensation. There is a dispute resolution procedure, with an appeal to the county court.

This new edition sets out the details of these provisions, and highlights a number of areas in which unanswered questions may lead to difficulties.

The other contents of the book have also been revised. The important topic of determining and contesting boundaries is rarely subject to major changes, but there is a steady flow of court decisions adding to and clarifying the law. The recently reported ones have been incorporated into the book, together with the implications of a number of statutes which touch on relevant topics.

The new Act is treated as in force; otherwise the law is stated as at 1 November 1996.

Chapter 1

Determining Boundaries

1 Construing title deeds

(a) Parcels

Parcels of land in separate ownership may be divided horizontally, vertically or in any other way (Law of Property Act ('LPA') 1925, s 205(1)(ix)). As this power is unrestricted, the first consideration in determining boundaries is to look at the acts of the owners of the different parcels as revealed by the title deeds. A clear definition in the deeds will normally be conclusive. To this general rule there are a number of exceptions.

First, adverse occupation by a squatter for a sufficient time to acquire title under the Limitation Act 1980 may alter the boundary. Secondly, an act of the landowner or one of his predecessors in title, although not varying the boundary shown on his deeds, may estop him from taking action in respect of the infringement. Thirdly, if the title deeds to the adjoining properties conflict, then reference will have to be made to the deeds showing the original division.

The limitation on the commencement of title in s 44 of the LPA 1925 (as amended by the LPA 1969, s 23), applies to matters between vendor and purchaser, and would not bar an older deed being adduced in evidence in a boundary dispute. Similarly, because of the general rule that Land Registry plans do not necessarily show precise boundaries, reference may need to be made in cases of registered title to pre-registration deeds.

Fourthly, a deed containing an error by both parties to it, or not accurately representing their prior agreement, will normally be rectified by the court, unless the applicant has disentitled himself to equitable relief, eg by laches. Fifthly, the boundary may subsequently be varied by statute, although evidence of this should have been placed with or indorsed upon the deeds.

(b) Ambiguity

If the definition of the parcels is clear, and yet some further erroneous description is added to it, the latter may be disregarded, applying the maxim *falsa demonstratio non nocet*. This applies where a deed defines boundaries by reference to existing physical objects, and also states the area of the land, and the two descriptions disagree. The description by physical objects will prevail. Thus, if a lease of land describes the premises by admeasurement and adds 'with the houses now erected or being erected thereon' and the foundations have already been laid and extend beyond the boundaries according to the measurements, the description by measurements is disregarded and the boundaries extend to include the foundations (*Manning v Fitzgerald* (1859) 29 LJ Ex 24). The maxim applied in that case to reject the first description.

Another example of the application of the maxim is a case where land was described in a tabulated schedule to a conveyance. The second column, headed 'description', referred to a plan which clearly showed an area conveyed of 27 perches. The fourth column of the schedule gave the area as 34 perches. The larger figure, coming second, was treated as erroneous and disregarded (*Llewellyn v Earl of Jersey* (1843) 11 M & W 183).

Should there be a number of conflicting descriptions, however, the maxim *falsa demonstratio non nocet* is not available to permit all but the first to be discarded. The order is not in that case paramount (*Eastwood v Ashton* [1915] AC 900). Which description prevails is a question of construction; there are no general presumptions.

It is sometimes possible to admit extrinsic evidence of the parties' intentions, eg that both landlord and tenant meant to include a rear storeroom when they only referred to a shop (*IS Mills (Yardley) Ltd v Curdworth Investments Ltd* [1975] 2 EGLR 54).

(c) Descriptive words

Certain words have acquired a technical meaning, and where they occur in a description of property they can assist in defining the boundaries. 'Messuage' and 'house' both pass a dwellinghouse with its curtilage, attached garden and buildings appurtenant to it. 'Dwellinghouse' is not limited to the part of the building that happens to be occupied for residential purposes (*Grigsby v Melville* [1974] 1 WLR 80). 'Curtilage' means land that belongs to a house in the physical sense. The term can be used for the land that goes with

other buildings, eg a church (*Re St John's Church, Bishop's Hatfield*
[1967] P 113). Land is sometimes described as having a building
erected on it 'or on some part thereof'. This implies that more than
the mere site of the building is referred to (*Bisney v Swanston*
(1973) 225 EG 2299).

'Farm' passes the farmhouse and the land held with it. 'Water'
passes the right to water and fishing, but not the land beneath it.
'Pool' passes both the water and its bed.

Where it is clear that the intention of the deed is to convey the
whole of the grantor's holding, evidence of the extent of that
holding will be admitted to construe the deed (*Maxted v Plymouth
Corporation* [1957] CLY 243). If all but a small part of the grantor's
land is conveyed and no intention to retain any has been displayed
(as where the title deeds are handed over), the whole plot with its
original boundaries will be presumed to be conveyed, in the
absence of contrary evidence.

The position of a fence may itself determine the interpretation in
the context of a 'close' or 'curtilage' (*Walsh v Allweather
Mechanical Grouting Co Ltd* [1959] 2 QB 300: not a case interpreting a title deed).

(d) General words

The general words implied into the description of the parcels in
a conveyance by s 62 of the LPA 1925 can extend the amount of
property which appears to be conveyed, and therefore affects its
boundary. In a case where the parcels were described in the deed
and shown coloured on a plan, part of a yard which was not
coloured was conveyed because one of the general words was 'yard'
and was held to include it (*Willis v Watney* (1881) 51 LJ Ch 588).

2 Plans

A plan referred to may be drawn on or annexed to the deed,
form part of another deed or be independent of the title, eg an
Ordnance Survey or tithe map. If the plan is to be of assistance, it
will have to be sufficiently clear and detailed to be self-
explanatory.

(a) Ordnance Survey

Ordnance Survey practice, where there are boundary features
such as hedges or fences between parcels of land, is to draw the

FIGURE 1.1

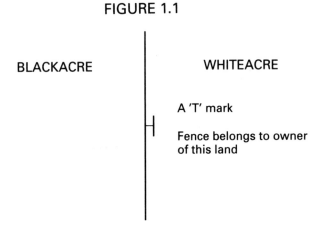

boundary line down the middle of these features. General presumptions, which may suggest that the boundary should lie down one side or the other, are ignored. This will apply to plans which do not explicitly state that they are extracts from, or based upon, the Ordnance Survey, but which can be seen to be so (eg because the Ordnance Survey parcel numbers are given).

(b) 'T' and 'H' marks

It is the practice to define the ownership of boundary features, or the responsibility for their maintenance, by inserting 'T' marks. The convention is that the 'T' is written, with its cross stroke parallel to the boundary and its down stroke touching it, on the side of the boundary on which lies the property with which the feature is included (see Figure 1.1.). There is no authority to suggest that this is anything more than a convention.

If, as sometimes happens, 'T' marks appear on the plan without any reference to them in the deed, they can be no more than persuasive evidence of the ownership of the boundary features. Since 1962 'T' marks have been shown on the filed plan of land with registered title in certain circumstances (p 24). This does not, however, invest them with any greater significance than they would have when considering the precise position of the boundary of unregistered land.

FIGURE 1.2

BLACKACRE   WHITEACRE

An 'H' mark

Indicates a party wall

Occasionally, an 'H' mark will be found, but much less frequently than 'T' marks. The 'H' is written so that its vertical strokes are parallel to the boundary, one on each side of it, so that it is, in effect, two 'T' marks joined. This is intended to indicate a party wall (see Figure 1.2.). Because of the ambiguity of that expression (see Chapter 4), and because 'H' marks are not used frequently enough for a universal practice to have been established, they cannot be regarded as of any evidential value if they appear without any verbal explanation.

(c) Effect on parcels

An incomplete verbal description of premises in a deed may be supplemented by reference to any plan to which the deed refers. Indeed, it has been said 'where parcels in a conveyancing document are described by reference to a plan attached to the document, the natural inference is that it was the intention that anyone concerned should see from the document alone, which means from the plan on it, what land the document was purporting to pass' (*AJ Dunning & Sons (Shopfitters) Ltd v Sykes & Son (Poole) Ltd* [1987] 1 All ER 700, 706 per Dillon LJ). Where the wording of the conveyance is ambiguous, a plan annexed to the conveyance, even if not referred to, may be considered (*Leachman v L & K Richardson Ltd* [1969] 1 WLR 1129).

Should the verbal description of the parcels and the plan disagree, it is a question of construction of the deed's reference to the plan, to determine which will prevail. It may be possible to adduce extrinsic evidence (*Scarfe v Adams* [1981] 1 All ER 843). When the words are not clear, but go on to define the property as 'more particularly described' on the plan, the latter will prevail (*Eastwood v Ashton* [1915] AC 900).

The plan may influence the construction of the words of the deed. A house described as 'comprising that portion of Terrant Monkton House which was formerly known as the Old Rectory' was not restricted to what had been the Old Rectory when more was shown on the plan. 'Comprising' was construed as 'including' (*Smout v Farquharson* (1973) 226 EG 114). Where there is no conflict between the description and the plan, even a plan for identification can supplement the verbal description (*Tebaldi v Wiseman and Kemp* (1983) 133 NLJ 1042: the plan on a lease of a basement flat showed that the internal staircase down to it was included in the demise).

The maxim *falsa demonstratio non nocet* can apply here also. Where the deed's description makes it clear that the boundary runs along the centre line of a hedge, but adds 'which said piece of land is delineated on the plan drawn hereon' and the plan shows the boundary lines at the foot of the hedge, the plan is ignored and the boundary is in the middle of the hedge (*Maxted v Plymouth Corporation* [1957] CLY 243). On the other hand, if, as a matter of construction, the description of the property in the parcels of a conveyance is to be read as a whole, dimensions given in the verbal description can prevail over an inaccurate plan (*Boyd Gibbins Ltd v Hockham* (1966) 199 EG 229). Where the title to land is registered, a conflict between the verbal description of the land and the filed plan for that title number, or the general map, may be resolved by the Registrar, subject to an appeal to the High Court (Land Registration Rules 1925, r 285).

(d) For identification only

In principle, a plan which the deed states to be 'for identification only' should be used to show the general location of the land, but not its precise extent (*Moreton C Cullimore (Gravels) Ltd v Routledge* (1977) 121 SJ 202). Nevertheless, it can supplement a verbal description which is not clear (*Wiggington & Milner Ltd v Winster Engineering Ltd* [1978] 1 WLR 1462; *Hatfield v Moss* [1988]

2 EGLR 58) or does not answer all the problems (*Targett v Ferguson* (1996) 72 P&CR 106). The surrounding physical circumstances can also be taken into account where it is necessary to resort to a plan expressed to be for identification only, eg the position of a boundary pegged out on the ground (*Willson v Greene* [1971] 1 WLR 635).

A plan 'for identification only' is said not to be acceptable for Land Registry purposes. No rule expressly prohibits such references, but the view is that such a plan does not define the land dealt with sufficiently precisely. Nevertheless, experience suggests that there are in fact many registered leases—which, unlike transfers, do not have to be in a prescribed form—with plans referred to in this way.

A plan stated to be 'for the purposes of delineation only' is one not true to scale (*Re Freeman and Taylor's Contract* (1907) 97 LT 39).

3 Presumptions in certain cases

Where the boundaries of land are defined by reference to, or in fact follow, certain physical features, advantage may be taken of legal presumptions applicable to land bounded by such features, which will apply unless or until rebutted by contrary evidence (*Beaufort (Duke) v Swansea Corporation* (1849) 3 Exch 413). In one case, a plan prepared for an auction some 75 years earlier provided such contrary evidence (*Falkingham v Farley* (1991) *The Times*, 11 March). It must be emphasised that these presumptions may be modified or excluded where the title to the land is registered, and reference should be made to pp 23–25. Assistance may also be gained from statutory rules where the adjoining property is used for certain purposes. Listed alphabetically below are a number of features by which boundaries may be defined, with particulars of whether, and if so, what special rules apply in each case.

(a) Beach

'Beach' is not a term of art. When used to define a boundary it may *prima facie* have the same meaning as 'seashore' (*Government of State of Penang v Beng Hong Oon* [1972] AC 425). However, it can extend further—to include land in apparent continuity with the beach at high water mark, ie until there is a change of vegetation, a physical barrier, or a road (*Tito v Waddell (No 2)* [1977] Ch 106, 263).

(b) Canals

Artificial waterways are not subject to the presumptions noted below in respect of certain rivers, where the riparian lands extend to the centre of the stream, because they must have been originally dug by a person on his own land or on land acquired from the adjoining owners for the purpose. Land bordering a canal is bounded by it, so minerals beneath the canal do not pass on a conveyance of the bordering land which does not expressly include the canal, or some part of it, even though they belong to the transferor (*Chamber Colliery Co v Rochdale Canal Co* [1895] AC 564).

(c) Flats

A part of a house, divided horizontally or vertically, which is leased separately includes the external walls enclosing that part, unless there are provisions to the contrary in the lease. A covenant by the landlord to do external repairs is not sufficient to displace this presumption (*Sturge v Hackett* [1962] 1 WLR 1257). The outside of a flat can be expressly excluded from a demise of it, but that does not prevent the external walls from constituting its exterior for the purposes of the landlord's implied repairing obligations (*Campden Hill Towers Ltd v Gardner* [1977] QB 823).

(d) Foreshore

See (*q*) *Seashore*, below.

(e) Forests

The boundaries of the royal forests—most of which were vested in the Minister of Agriculture and Fisheries (now the Minister of Agriculture, Fisheries and Food) by the Forestry Act 1945—were finally fixed, after considerable friction between the Crown and its subjects, by the Delimitation of Forests Act 1640. This necessarily also fixed the boundaries of the private lands adjoining the forests. Since then, however, considerable areas have been disafforested by special statutes, private inclosure acts, and letters patent. These have mostly passed into private ownership.

FIGURE 1.3

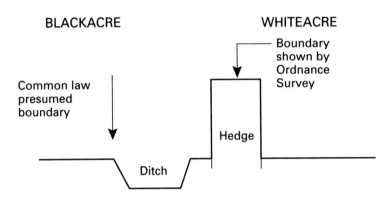

(f) Hedges and ditches

Where two fields are separated by an artificial ditch alongside a bank, with or without a hedge or fence on it, there is a presumption that the boundary is along the edge of the ditch furthest from the bank (*Fisher v Winch* [1939] 1 KB 666). This is because it is assumed that the landowner digs his drainage ditch on the extreme edge of his property and throws up the earth on to his own side of the ditch to avoid committing a trespass against his neighbour. This forms the bank upon which he plants a hedge or erects a fence (*Vowles v Miller* (1810) 3 Taunt 137, 138 per Lawrence J). The presumption only applies to a single hedge (or fence or bank) and ditch. If there is one without the other, or two hedges or two ditches, no such presumption operates, because the original landowner's actions in digging the ditch or planting the hedge cannot be logically deduced. Similarly, because the presumption is based on a landowner's action in digging the ditch, it probably does not apply where the ditch is natural and not artificial (*Marshall v Taylor* [1895] 1 Ch 641, 647).

Although this is only a presumption, a conveyance which purports to convey land which did not belong to the seller does not displace it (*Hall v Docling* [1996] EGCS 58).

Ordnance Survey practice is to take the centre line of the hedge as the boundary (see Figure 1.3.). Judicial notice of this practice has been taken in a consistory court (*Re St Peter and St Paul,*

Scrayingham [1992] 1 WLR 187). A conveyance which describes the land conveyed by express reference to the Ordnance Survey will rebut the presumption, in favour of the Ordnance Survey practice (*Rouse v Gravel-works Ltd* [1940] 1 KB 489 (at first instance); *Davey v Harrow Corporation* [1958] 1 QB 60). It is thought, however, that the presumption would still be applied where the conveyance plan was based on the Ordnance Survey for convenience, without expressly incorporating the Survey map.

(g) Highways

If a highway is fenced on both sides, it will be presumed to extend up to both fences (or hedges). But this only applies if it can be shown that the fences were erected (or hedges planted) to separate the adjoining closes from the highway (*Attorney-General v Beynon* [1970] Ch 1). The presumption extends to land between other boundary features, eg banks, whether natural or man-made (*Naydler v Hampshire County Council* (1973) 226 EG 176) but it was rebutted where it was shown that the fence predated the highway (*Minting v Ramage* [1991] EGCS 12).

There are said to be two occasions on which a presumption arises as to the boundary of land adjoining a highway. First, the boundary of land adjoining a highway is presumed to be a line drawn down the middle of the highway, and land 'adjoins' a highway for this purpose although separated from it by a public right of way not being part of the street (*Ware Urban District Council v Gaunt* [1960] 1 WLR 1364). This presumption only applies where the conveyancing history of the land and the road is unknown (*Giles v County Building Constructors (Hertford) Ltd* (1971) 22 P & CR 978, 981).

For the purpose of making up and adopting private roads, road charges are normally imposed on the owners of property 'fronting' (which includes 'adjoining': Highways Act 1980, s 203(3)) the street (s 205). An upper maisonette, separated from the highway by a 25 foot garden belonging to the lower maisonette, does not adjoin the highway for this purpose (*Buckinghamshire County Council v Trigg* [1963] 1 WLR 155). But leaving a 12 foot strip of land between a housing development and the road, to accommodate future widening, does not prevent the houses fronting the road (*Warwickshire County Council v Adkins* (1967) 112 SJ 135).

The second case in which there may be a presumption is on the conveyance of land forming part of a building estate. It can include half the road, even though it clearly describes the property as excluding any part of the road. Very little now seems to be needed to rebut this presumption (*Giles v County Building Constructors (Hertford) Ltd* (1971) 22 P&CR 978).

The surface of that part of the land comprising the highway is not normally vested in the adjoining owner, but the boundary is important in passing the ground beneath the surface with its minerals and possible basement accommodation. In such a case, the ownership of growing trees remains in the owner of the subsoil, although the management and control of them may be assumed by the highway authority (*Russell v London Borough of Barnet* [1984] 2 EGLR 44).

The boundary also needs to be considered where a stopping-up order is obtained so that the surface reverts to private ownership. In some cases where the land was conveyed to the highway authority (not dedicated), a stopping-up order will only extinguish the public rights over the surface, the land remaining vested in the highway authority. The boundaries are then unaffected. Where only part of a highway is affected by a stopping-up order it is thought that this does not affect the position of the boundary, which thereafter need not be in the centre of the remaining road. The boundary is fixed on the first conveyance of the land, and all that is changed are the rights that may be exercised over part of the surface of the plot. Where it is not practicable to trace the original conveyance, such evidence of the facts as is available will have to be relied upon. Statutory declarations as to the practice in the past made by independent persons would normally be accepted in a conveyancing transaction; evidence admissible in court is considered below, at pp 35–42.

In the case of registered land the half of the highway is excluded from the registration of the title of the adjoining land if adopted by the local authority. This was started as an application of the general boundaries rule (pp 23–24), and applied even in cases of an express conveyance of half the roadway. However, it is now clear that where the highway authority has the surface vested in it, it acquires a legal estate (*Tithe Redemption Commission v Runcorn Urban District Council* [1954] Ch 383), so it would not be proper to do otherwise. The presumption still applies to the subsoil.

The presumption of ownership of half an adjoining highway is displaced by evidence showing an intention not to include any part of the road. In one case, the presumption did not apply where a sewer was to be laid under the road by the authority leasing the adjoining land, and there was even doubt whether they had power to include it (*Mappin Brothers v Liberty & Co Ltd* [1903] 1 Ch 118).

(h) Houses

Where a house is conveyed or demised there is a presumption that it passes in its entirety, including projecting eaves and footings (although not shown on the plan referred to), but not the air space between them (*Truckwell v Stock* [1957]1 WLR 161). On the other hand, a conveyance of property by reference to the ground plan of a building will include part of a neighbouring building which overhangs above it (*Laybourne v Gridley* [1892] 2 Ch 53). A conveyance of a dwellinghouse by description passed with it a void under the ground floor, even though the only access to that basement was from the adjoining property, with which it had previously been enjoyed (*Grigsby v Melville* [1974] 1 WLR 80).

Walls which are shared by two properties (eg those between semidetached or terraced houses) may belong to one of the adjoining houses exclusively if there is clear evidence that the wall is on one side of the boundary line. It is usual, however, for them to be party walls (Chapter 4), and in the absence of contrary evidence there is a presumption that the boundary runs down the middle of the wall.

Where land is conveyed described as bounded by a house, or something else to which title would normally be made independently, the boundary object is completely excluded.

(i) Islands

Ownership of the bank of a non-tidal river does not carry with it islands up to a line midway between the two banks. The riparian owner's boundary is in the middle of the stream between the bank and the island (*Great Torrington Commons Conservators v Moore Stevens* [1904] 1 Ch 347). There is no settled presumption, however, on the line of the boundary round the ends of the island facing up and down stream (see Figure 1.4.).

The boundary of an island is similarly in the middle of the stream. If the title to the island is registered, with the boundary shown at the water's edge, the presumption applies. It is not displaced by a claim to a corporeal fishery over more than half the stream, because being land it would itself have to be registered (*Hesketh v Willis Cruisers Ltd* (1968) 19 P & CR 573).

FIGURE 1.4

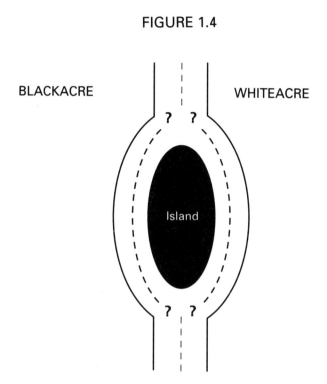

Two banks of river and an island, each in separate ownership.

By presumption, the boundary lies midstream between the two river banks, or the bank and the island.

How the boundary runs at the end of the island is unclear.

The position is different when islands are formed by the water suddenly cutting off what was formerly part of the bank, or laying bare land formerly covered by water. Those islands belong to the riparian owners, the boundary being drawn where it was before the islands were formed. In tidal rivers, islands created by uncovering the river bed (even if only at low tide), or to which the riparian owners or some other person cannot make title, belong to the Crown. If part of a riparian owner's land is suddenly cut off by the waters of a tidal river, his boundary remains unaltered and extends round the island.

There are no presumptions relating to islands in lakes.

(j) Lakes

There is no settled presumption about the position of the boundary between properties in different ownership separated by a lake. The question of whether a rule similar to that for rivers applies, was left undecided in a nineteenth century case (*Marshall v Ulleswater Steam Navigation Co Ltd* (1863) 3 B & S 732, 742). Evidence of exclusive possession will normally be conclusive. A lake wholly within the boundaries of a parcel of land will pass without special reference, unless expressly excluded. Equally, a lake could be conveyed separately from any surrounding property, when its boundaries, if not defined, would probably be the water's edge at the normal water level.

Where land adjoining a lake is conveyed, the lake forms its boundary. Gradual accretions to the land, as a result of natural forces, become part of it. The boundary moves to the position of the edge of the lake for the time being (*Southern Centre of Theosophy Inc v State of South Australia* [1982] AC 706). Presumably, the same applies, in reverse, if the lake shore is eroded.

(k) Pipe-lines

The grant of an easement for a pipe or wire may give exclusive rights of use. The boundaries of the land over which the easement is granted do not extend beyond the physical extent of the pipe, etc, unless otherwise stated, but such an easement will automatically carry ancillary rights of entry for inspection, cleaning, repair and replacement (*Jones v Pritchard* [1908] 1 Ch 630). Land through which passes a pipeline authorised by the Pipelines Act 1962 may have been acquired by the pipe-line owner, or he may only have rights of user. A plan showing the route and extent of a pipe-line authorised to be laid or diverted under the Act must be deposited with the local authorities of the areas affected (s 35). This plan is open for inspection by anyone at all reasonable times without fee.

(l) Railways

No special presumption applies to railways. The boundary is where it appears to be and not in the centre of the track, because the land on which the railway is built had to be acquired from the adjoining owner and became a separate plot at that date. Adjoining landowners are therefore not automatically entitled to minerals under the railway (*Thompson v Hickman* [1907] 1 Ch 550). However, conveyances under the Railways Clauses Consolidation Act 1845, s 77, do not pass the mines and minerals unless expressly included, and they therefore remain vested in the grantor who may well be the adjoining owner. This section is taken to apply to Land Registry transfers where appropriate.

The boundary of a railway will usually be such as to include the boundary fence with the railway, by reason of the fencing obligations imposed on railway companies by the Railways Clauses Consolidation Act 1845, s 68. These obligations may not, however, apply: see p 73.

(m) Rights of way

Where a private right of way forms a boundary, the same presumption arises as for highways, ie the centre line of the path or roadway is the boundary (*Lang v House* (1961) 178 EG 801). But in this case the land up to the half-way line remains vested in the adjoining owners (subject only to the rights of way), and will not be excluded from a registered title. The extent of the right of way itself may depend on the use to which it is put. A reservation which included the passage of cattle extended beyond the metalled road to include the verges (*Haynes v Brassington* [1988] EGCS 100).

(n) Rivers

In the case of non-tidal rivers, the boundary of the riparian lands is presumed to be in the centre of the stream. This presumption extends to the river Tweed where it forms the boundary between England and Scotland (*Lovett v Fairclough* (1990) 61 P & CR 385).

... Where land adjoining ... [an] inland river is granted, the *prima facie* presumption is, that the parties intended to include in the grant a moiety ... of the river bed ... ; and that such general presumption ought to prevail, unless there is something to indicate a contrary intention (*Dwyer v Rich* (1871) Ir Rep 6 Ch 144, 149).

A contrary intention may be shown by one riparian owner performing acts of ownership. This was so in one case where he exercised them lower down the stream at a point where the other bank was a third party's property (*Jones v Williams* (1837) 2 M&W 326).

The presumption applies not only on the conveyance of freehold land bounded by a river, but also on the grant of a lease of such land (*Tilbury v Silva* (1890) 45 Ch D 98, 109 per Kay J). The same rule applies to the limits of riparian owners' fishing rights in Scotland (*Fothringham v Kerr* (1984) 48 P & CR 173). The presumption is not displaced by the fact that the grantor owns both banks of the river nor by facts, which only came to light later which, had they been known, might have induced him to reserve the river bed (*Micklethwait v Newlay Bridge Co* (1886) 23 Ch D 133).

When the river and the adjoining bank are each conveyed separately without the boundary being defined, the division is at the water's edge (*Bridden v Fenn* [1986] CLY 2830 (CC)). If there is evidence that the river and its bed belong to some person other than the riparian owners, this rebuts the presumption. The boundary is the water line when the river is in its natural state, disregarding seasonal fluctuations. Evidence of independent ownership would be either normal conveyancing evidence of title, long possession as of right, or acts of ownership (*Jones v Williams* (1837) 2 M&W 326).

If there are gradual, imperceptible accretions to either bank in the ordinary course of nature, the additional land belongs to that riparian owner and the boundary in the centre of the stream is automatically adjusted, even though the original boundary may still be ascertainable (*Foster v Wright* (1878) 4 CPD 438). If, however, the river suddenly completely changes its course, the boundary remains where it was immediately before the diversion (*Ford v Lacy* (1861) 7 H & N 151). When two riparian owners in Scotland agreed to divert the river defining their boundary, the result was to draw the boundary along the new course of the river (*Stirling v Bartlett* (1992) *The Times*, 29 October).

The soil of the bed of a river where it is tidal *prima facie* belongs to the Crown (being managed by the Crown Estate Commissioners) (Coast Protection Act 1949), except in the cases of the rivers Thames and Tees). It continues to do so even if the river gradually changes course (*Carlisle Corporation v Graham* (1869) LR 4 Ex 361). The boundary on each side is medium high water. Accordingly, the fishing on such stretches of river does not pass with the riparian lands, as it normally does on non-tidal waters.

(o) Roads

See (g) *Highways*, above.

(p) Rooms

Where a room is demised without any precise definition of its boundaries, the position varies according to whether its walls constitute outside walls of the building, or partition walls. The whole of any outside wall is included, but only an undefined part of a partition wall passes with the room (*Phelps v City of London Corporation* [1916] 2 Ch 255, 263).

(q) Seashore

The technical name for the seashore is 'foreshore', but in an appropriate context, where this is meant, these words are synonymous (*Mellor v Walmesley* [1905] 2 Ch 164). The boundary between the seashore and the adjoining land is presumed to be the line of medium high tide between the ordinary spring and neap tides (*Attorney-General v Chambers* (1854) 4 De GM & G 206). The lower boundary of the seashore is the medium low water mark. In Scotland, the rule is that the boundary lies at the high water mark of the ordinary spring tides (*Mussleburgh Real Estate Co Ltd v Mussleburgh Provost* [1905] AC 491).

Nevertheless, if the evidence warrants, 'foreshore' can mean the whole of the shore from time to time exposed by the receding tide: the ordinary, everyday connotation of the word (*Loose v Castleton* (1978) 41 P&CR 19, 34 per Bridge LJ).

The 'low water line' is necessarily one which moves with the seasons. ' ... there is no established rule of law that the low water mark is necessarily the line of median low water, and the principle which identifies the landwards boundary of the foreshore at the line of median high water depends on factors which have no application to the seaward low water mark. Nor is there any general rule as to the meaning of "low water line" or "low water mark" ' (*Anderson v Alnwick District Council* [1993] 3 All ER 613, 620 per Evans LJ).

A conveyance of land described as bounded by the seashore, but containing measurements making it clear that there is a strip of land between that conveyed and the seashore, estops the grantor denying the grantee access to the seashore over that strip, but does not convey the strip (*Mellor v Walmesley*, above). If the medium high tide line moves, the boundary of land described as bounded by the seashore moves with it. This is a moveable freehold (*Scratton v Brown* (1825) 4 B & C 485; *Smart & Co v Suva Town Board* [1893] AC 301). This is the effect of imperceptible accretions to the shore, which add to the land in private ownership, or of gradual erosion which returns land to the ownership of the Crown (*Re Hull and Selby Railway* (1839) 5 M & W 139). The common law treats the land as if it had always, since the limit of legal memory, been as it now is (*Mercer v Denne* [1905] 2 Ch 538).

Whether land conveyed is in fact bounded by a moveable line, or whether the boundary is fixed in the place to which the tide came when the deed was executed, is a question of construction of the document (*Baxendale v Instow Parish Council* [1982] Ch 14). The fact that there are physical markers showing the boundary line in its original position does not necessarily prevent the boundary being altered by natural forces (*Attorney-General v M'Carthy* [1911] 2 IR 260).

Land reclaimed by the owner of land bounded by the sea does not belong to him, but to the Crown (*Attorney-General of Southern Nigeria v John Holt and Company (Liverpool) Ltd* [1915] AC 599).

(r) Waste land

Where a fenced close adjoins waste land, there is a presumption that the fence belongs to the owner of the close (*White v Taylor (No 2)* [1960] 1 Ch 160).

4 Other evidence of boundaries

Other forms of evidence of the position of boundaries may be available. These are discussed in Chapter 3 in relation to boundary disputes, where their admissibility in accordance with the strict rules of evidence is considered.

5 Horizontal boundaries

(a) Minerals

Although mines and minerals are readily severable from the surface of the land, there is normally no definition of the boundary between them and the surface. It would appear that the owner of the minerals can work any substance which comes within the definition of minerals and to which he is entitled (not eg coal), so long as it is below the surface. It may be noted that certain conveyances (including Land Registry transfers) exclude mines and minerals unless they are expressly included (under the Railways Clauses Consolidation Act 1845, s 77, and the Waterworks Clauses Act 1847, s 18).

(b) Highways

The rights of the public to use a highway extend only to the surface of it. ' "Street" ... includes the surface and so much of the depth as may be not unfairly used, as streets are used' (*Coverdale v Charlton* (1878) 4 QBD 104, 121, per Brett LJ). Or, as it was put earlier, ' ... the King has nothing but the passage for himself and his people: but the freehold and all profits belong to the owner of the soil. So do all the trees upon it, and mines under it ... ' (*Goodtitle v Alker* (1757) 1 Burr 133, 143 per Lord Mansfield). This defines the extent of the property of which the highway authority can make use. Those rights do not permit the use for other amenities, such as underground public conveniences, even though constructed by the highway authority (*Tunbridge Wells Corporation v Baird* [1896] AC 434). Statute may, however, confer rights on the highway or other authorities to construct under highways these and other amenities (eg car parks) which the common law would not permit. The highway authority has a legal estate in so much of the surface land as is vested in it for highway purposes. This is a determinable fee simple, lasting only while the use as a highway continues (*Tithe Redemption Commission v Runcorn Urban District Council* [1954] Ch 383).

(c) Streams

Although running water is not capable of being owned, a stream may be vested in a different person from its bed. A stream may eg be a public sewer, and so vested in a water company as successor to the water authority (Public Health Act 1936, s 20; Water Act 1973, Sched 8, para 33; repealed), while the bed remains the property of the riparian owners. The boundary between the bed and the stream above it is not subject to any legal presumption, but must be the place at which the liquid of the stream physically meets the solid substance of the bed.

(d) Basements

Basements of premises adjoining streets built lying under the street can extend up to the horizontal boundary between the highway and the subsoil. Where the basement has existed for some time this will be excellent evidence of the lowest possible limit of the surface in cases where the highway authority later wishes to extend its occupation downwards. Although roads adopted by the local authority are excluded from registered titles, basements under them will be included in the registration if the position is made clear to the Land Registry. Where they have not been so included, they are taken to pass on dispositions of the registered land under the Land Registration Rules 1925, r 251, which passes all rights, etc enjoyed with the land.

(e) Flats and maisonettes

There are no settled presumptions determining the horizontal boundary of a flat (or maisonette) from the one above or below it. However, 'it is the general expectation of anyone who takes the lease of a flat that he acquires the space between the floor of his flat and the underneath of the floor of the flat above' (*Graystone Property Investments Ltd v Margulies* (1983) 47 P & CR 472, 474, per Griffiths LJ).

The terms of the lease demising the property may, by implication, help to decide the point. So, an express demise of the roof carried with it the air above (*Davies v Yadegar* [1990] 1 EGLR 70). The same applied where there was an express restriction on improvements carried out there (*Haines v Florensa* [1990] 1 EGLR 73) and the roof was included in the demise where there was an express obligation to repair it (*Straudley Investments Ltd v Barpress Ltd* [1987] 1 EGLR 69).

The Court of Appeal has accepted that the upper boundary is not lower than the underside of the floor joists to which the ceiling is fixed, but it left undecided the question whether in fact the flat extends upwards to half-way through the joists, or even to the upperside of them (*Sturge v Hackett* [1962] 1 WLR 1257, 1266). In particular circumstances, a flat included a void created by false suspended ceilings which were lower than the original ceilings (*Graystone Property Investments Ltd v Margulies*, above). The demise of a top floor flat may, but does not necessarily, include the roof space above it (*Hatfield v Moss* [1988] 2 EGLR 58) and even the roof. Whether it does is a matter of construction of the document (*Cockburn v Smith* [1924] 2 KB 119).

Where the lower boundary is not defined, at least some part of the floor is included (*Phelps v City of London Corporation* [1916] 2 Ch 255, 264).

The divisions are sometimes referred to as 'party floors' or 'party ceilings'. In the case of party walls there is a presumption in the absence of contrary evidence that the boundary runs down the middle, but it is doubtful whether this applies to floors and ceilings. Some of the provisions of the Party Wall etc Act 1996 may apply. But the provisions of the LPA 1925, s 38, do not; they do not envisage hollow structures which most floors and ceilings are, and they only deal with a vertical division.

(*f*) *Building with air beneath*

In the unusual case of a building suspended over air in separate ownership—eg a first floor building with an open passage way underneath—the whole of the building's lower wall, including brick vaulting, belongs to the owner of the building (*Cresswell v Duke of Westminster* [1985] 2 EGLR 151).

6 Registered land

(*a*) *General boundaries*

In the absence of special notes on the register, dealt with below under the heading (b) *Fixed boundaries*, the boundaries on the Land Registry general map and filed plans of particular titles indicate only general boundaries (Land Registration Rules 1925, r 278). That is to say, although it may be clear that some physical feature is followed—such as a wall or a ditch—the exact position of the line on the plan does not indicate who owns the feature, or whether the boundary actually runs down one of the sides or down the middle of it.* As the Land Registry maps and plans often consist of or are based on Ordnance Survey maps, the boundary lines will normally be drawn down the middle of the physical features in accordance with the Ordnance Survey practice. A broken line is often used on the Registry plans to indicate a boundary where no physical feature yet exists, as where a fence is

---

* This sentence was cited in *Cutland v Atwell* (1994) unreported, per Peter Gibson LJ.

still to be erected. Nevertheless, Land Registry plans are as precise as possible and no great variation from the boundary shown comes within the rule. *Lee v Barrey* [1957] Ch 251, where the Court of Appeal held that a divergence of ten feet was within the general boundaries rule, is considered exceptional. That particular filed plan bore an endorsement that it was subject to revision after the erection of fences, implying that it gave no more than a general indication of the boundaries.

Without being technically fixed boundaries, certain boundary features may be recorded on the register as either included in or excluded from the title. These precise indications are effective, but leave the general rule unaffected as far as the rest of the boundaries are concerned.

The filed plan may show 'T' marks in two circumstances. First, when they are referred to in restrictive covenants, or in positive covenants imposed with restrictive ones and reproduced on the register with them. Secondly, in cases where they appeared on a plan referred to in a pre-registration deed, but without any explanation in the deed of their significance, and the applicant for first registration specifically requests their inclusion. In the latter case, the fact that the marks were not referred to in the deed will be recorded on the register. Before 1962 such 'T' marks were not reproduced on filed plans.

(b) *Fixed boundaries*

Only where there is a note in the property register that the boundaries have been fixed, and also on the filed plan or general map, will the boundaries be precise and fixed (Land Registration Rules 1925, r 277). The obvious advantages are that those boundaries can be relied upon, and are guaranteed so that even the slightest adjustment by rectification could be the basis of an indemnity claim under the Land Registration Act 1925, s 83 (except in certain cases of acquisition by adverse possession). Application for registration with fixed boundaries must be made specifically to the Chief Land Registrar (there is no prescribed form), and may apply to part only of the boundary of a plot of land. Upon receipt of the application the Chief Land Registrar must give notice of the intention to ascertain and fix the boundaries, with a plan or description of the land, to the owners and occupiers of the adjoining lands (Land Registration Rules 1925, r 276). The freehold and leasehold titles of the owners of all adjoining lands to which the title is not registered will have to be deduced. A comprehensive and very accurate survey will then be undertaken. Disputes or questions of doubt may be resolved by hearings before the Chief Land Registrar, with a right of appeal to the High Court. An application for fixing boundaries can be extremely and disproportionately expensive, and the applicant can and will be called upon to pay all costs involved in serving notices, examining titles and surveying. There is no limit on this liability and an advance payment on account is normally required. Probably for this reason, and because fixed boundaries do not often offer many practical advantages, applications to have boundaries fixed are extremely rare.

7 Commons

The registration of common land and town and village greens under the Commons Registration Act 1965 involved a determination of their boundaries, and consequently the boundaries of the adjoining private properties. Registrations are by reference to plans, and the documents are open to public inspection. The register is conclusive evidence of the matters registered, as at the date of registration (s 10). This includes the extent of the land. The boundary of land to be registered as waste land of a manor does not alter, when bounded by the sea, when gradual imperceptible accretions change the shore line (*Baxendale v Instow Parish Council* [1982] Ch 14).

See the position as to the boundary of waste land (p 20).

8 Variation of boundaries

(*a*) *By agreement*

Adjoining landowners may fix or alter their boundaries by agreement. A variation of boundaries amounts to an assurance of the land involved. A deed is therefore necessary (LPA 1925, s 52), and if the title is registered the prescribed form of Land Registry transfer must be used. An agreement to complete a deed of variation or a transfer for this purpose must be in writing and comply with the requirements of the Law of Property (Miscellaneous Provisions) Act 1989, s 2. The only restrictions on the power of a landowner to agree to alter his boundaries are those general restrictions on any disposition of land imposed on certain bodies, or persons under a disability.

If, however, the boundary was previously in doubt, and the

agreement is a genuine attempt to state what is thought always to have been the position, neither a deed, nor even writing, is necessary because no land changes hands. For the same reason the agreement is not registrable as an estate contract under the Land Charges Act 1972, unless it intends to vary a boundary (*Neilson v Poole* (1969) 20 P & CR 909). The settlement is sufficient mutual consideration to make the agreement enforceable (*Penn v Lord Baltimore* (1750) 1 Ves Sen 444). Clearly, however, a deed accurately recording the settled boundaries for the future is more satisfactory.

(b) Limitation Act

All encroachment upon neighbouring land which lasts for 12 years and which fulfils the requirements of the Limitation Act for adverse possession inconsistent with the owner's title, completely extinguishes the former owner's right to the land (unless the title is registered) (Limitation Act 1980, s 15(1)). That varies the boundary (*Williams Bros Direct Supply Ltd v Raftery* [1958] QB 159). This applies even if the owner's right to recover possession is subject to statutory restriction (eg under the Rent Act) (*Moses v Lovegrove* [1952] 2 QB 533). Acquisition by prescription can vary the presumptions to which reference may be made when determining boundaries (eg where there is a hedge and a ditch) (*Marshall v Taylor* [1895] 1 Ch 641). But if the acts of purported ownership are not sufficient to establish adverse possession, a fence can lawfully be re-erected along the original boundary (*Dear v Woods* (1984) 9 CSW 728).

The Limitation Act extends the 12 year period in certain cases (Sched 1, Pt 2). The Crown or a spiritual or eleemosynary corporation sole has 30 years to bring an action. This is extended to 60 years for an action by the Crown to recover foreshore.

Where the title to the land concerned is registered, the former owner remains registered proprietor, holding in trust for the squatter (Land Registration Act 1925, s 75). Upon application, the register will be rectified to show the squatter as proprietor, and the plans will be varied as necessary. Until this is done the boundaries of the registered properties remain unaltered. A purchaser of registered land should accordingly inspect the property in the usual way before contracting: he cannot assume that all the land included in a registered title is occupied, or even beneficially owned, by the registered proprietor.

(c) Estoppel

A landowner's act, or that of a predecessor in title, may stop him from taking action in respect of an encroachment upon his boundaries that has the practical effect of varying the boundaries, at any rate as between those parties and persons deriving title under them. So where a company which owned one of two adjacent plots agreed with the owner of the other to build a house and garage on it in such a position that the garage encroached upon the company's plot by between two and three feet, the company's successor in title could not maintain an action for trespass against a subsequent owner of the garage (*Hopgood v Brown* [1955] 1 WLR 213).

(d) Rectification

Where the parties to a binding agreement purport to carry it into effect by a document which is not in accordance with the agreement, that document can be rectified. This principle can apply to vary boundaries of land defined by a conveyance, if they do not accord with what the parties agreed in their prior contract (*Craddock Brothers Ltd v Hunt* [1923] 2 Ch 136).

(e) Inclosure Acts

The inclosure of commons, which necessarily involves the definition of new boundaries, is not a subject that can be dealt with here. It must be mentioned, nevertheless, that a valuer appointed under the Inclosure Act 1845 has power, with the consent of adjoining owners, to straighten fences or define new boundaries of the lands to be inclosed or regulated, and to give directions for the fencing of the new boundary (s 45). This procedure is, however, virtually obsolete because it is extremely elaborate, including calling local meetings and promoting a private Act of Parliament. Other provisions in the many statutes governing inclosure can affect boundaries. They are administered by the Department of the Environment, who may be able to give help.

(f) Registered land

The boundaries of land to which title is registered can only be varied if the alteration is shown on the register. A plan or verbal description of registered land may be renewed, revised or corrected at any time. The proprietor must apply to the Registrar in writing, providing such evidence and serving such notices as he requires

(Land Registration Rules 1925, r 284(1)). The Registrar may vary boundaries under his powers of rectification (in default of a normal transfer). This power is conferred by the Land Registration Act 1925, s 82, to give effect to orders of the court, to alter entries obtained by fraud, to give effect to an agreement of all interested parties and to correct any error or omission. As has been noted, there is also power to give effect to an acquisition by adverse possession under the Limitation Act 1980. Cases of dispute will be dealt with in Chapter 3. Where all parties are in agreement, rectification of the register may well prove to be more simple than drawing the necessary deeds for an unregistered title, where the mapping is generally less accurate. Cases of errors in boundaries on the part of the Registry will give rise to claims for indemnity, unless they are so slight as to come within the general boundaries rule where that applies. This rule is not thought to permit any substantial variation from the line shown, although there is no definite scale that can be applied and presumably the latitude allowed would vary according to the circumstances of the case (eg greater variation could be expected on open moorland than in a built-up city). Where the Ordnance Survey map of the area is revised, the Land Registry maps based on it will normally be revised too, and a claim might also arise unless it was a case of showing more accurately the facts which always existed.

(g) Natural forces

The gradual effects of wind and tide can alter the position of a boundary which is defined by reference to a physical feature such as a river bank or seashore. This does not apply where a single unusually violent natural phenomenon drastically and suddenly alters the position of river bed (*Ford v Lacey* (1861) 7 H & N 151), but merely to imperceptible accretions. Those accretions can, however, be large enough to provide an easily measurable difference over, say, a year (*R v Lord Yarborough* (1824) 3 B & C 668).

The change in the position of the boundary applies equally to accretions and to erosion. Accretions to land bounded by the sea belong to the owner of that land (*Government of the State of Penang v Beng Hong Oon* [1972] AC 425), and erosion returns the land to Crown ownership (*Re Hull and Selby Railway* (1839) 5 M & W 139). The action of wind in blowing sand has been treated in the same way as alluvial accretions (*Southern Centre of Theosophy Inc v State of South Australia* [1982] AC 706).

Chapter 2

Sale of Land

1 Pre-contract

(a) Searches and enquiries

It is customary for prospective buyers to make preliminary enquiries of the seller as to the ownership of boundary features, and as to disputes which will include boundary disputes, unless details are volunteered by the seller on a property information form. Failure to disclose a dispute in reply to a preliminary enquiry can be a misrepresentation justifying the subsequent rescission of the contract (*Walker v Boyle* [1982] 1 WLR 495). A buyer's solicitor who fails to pursue enquiries to find the full facts about fences can be guilty of negligence (*McManus Developments Ltd v Barbridge Properties Ltd* [1992] EGCS 50).

Other pre-contract searches that can be important in relation to boundary features are:

(1) Ownership of fences adjoining a railway line: p 73.
(2) Whether the local planning authority has made a direction under art 4 of the Town and Country Planning General Development Order 1988, restricting the general permission given for the erection of fences etc (pp 83–4). One of the standard enquiries of local authorities to accompany local land charge searches refers to this, but it should be noted that it relates only to directions made by the council. In appropriate circumstances, a direction can be made by a joint planning board, an urban development corporation or an enterprise zone authority.

(b) *Misdescription*

Conveyancing contracts normally seek to restrict the purchaser's right to rescind on the ground of misrepresentation (eg *Standard Conditions of Sale*, 3rd edn, cond 7.1). How far such a condition is effective depends on the circumstances of each case. It must satisfy the test of reasonableness, ie the term must be a fair and reasonable one to be included having regard to the circumstances which were, or ought reasonably to have been, known to or in the contemplation of the parties when the contract was made (Misrepresentation Act 1967, s 3; Unfair Contract Terms Act 1977, ss 8(1), 11(1)).

In one case, auction particulars contained a colour photograph of the premises, wrongly showing the boundary to include too much property. The same conditions contained the term, 'The property is believed and should be taken to be accurately described ... and any error, omission or misstatement ... shall not annul the sale ... '. That clause did not prevent the buyer rescinding because the seller could not be said to have believed that the property was correctly described, and the term was not fair and reasonable (*St Marylebone Property Co Ltd v Payne* [1994] 2 EGLR 25 (CC)).

2 Title

(a) *Proof of extent of property*

A buyer has a right to a marketable title to the property sold by the contract, subject to any contrary terms in the contract. That involves establishing first the extent of what the seller contracts to sell, and secondly the boundaries of the land to which he deduces title. A contract normally defines the land sold in the particulars, and may refer to a plan. Even a plan which is not referred to in the contract may be used to determine what is sold, if it is handed to the purchaser with that intention (*Re Lindsay and Forder's Contract* (1895) 72 LT 832).

The courts are loath to deprive the buyer of his right to insist that the property to which title is offered is the same in extent as that which the seller contracted to sell. Contractual conditions which could prejudice that right are narrowly construed. In one case where the descriptions of the property in the various title deeds differed, and none was the same as the contract description, there was a condition of sale, 'that no further evidence of the identity of the parcels shall be required, than what is afforded by the abstract,

or the deeds, instruments, or other documents therein abstracted'.
Although the buyer could call for no further evidence, because of
the effect of that condition, the vendor had not fulfilled his obligation to identify what he was selling and so could not oblige the
purchaser to complete (*Flower v Hartopp* (1843) 6 Beav 476). In
another case, the contract provided that 'the purchaser is not to
require any further proof of identity than is furnished in the title
deeds themselves', but the deeds did not identify the property.
Again, the buyer could not require further evidence, but the seller
could not oblige him to buy (*Curling v Austin* (1862) 2 Dr & Sm
129).

A contract condition, in the National Conditions of Sale, 17th
edn, that the purchaser should admit the identity of the property
with that comprised in the documents of title on the evidence of the
descriptions in those deeds was considered in *Re Bramwell's
Contract, Bramwell v Ballards Securities Investments Ltd* [1969] 1
WLR 1659. The contract description of the property sold and the
parcels in the root of title could only be reconciled as a matter of
probability. As the deeds did not contain what could properly be
called a description of the property for the purpose of the condition,
it did not have any effect.

(b) Ownership of boundary features

Whether or not the seller owns the fences, etc, surrounding the
property sold will only have a very small effect on the extent of the
property sold, although disputes about ownership of and the
responsibility to maintain boundary features can lead to considerable acrimony. *The Standard Conditions of Sale*, 3rd edn, cond
4.3.1, provide:

The seller need not:
(a) prove the exact boundaries of the property
(b) prove who owns fences, ditches, hedges or walls ... further that he may
     be able to do from the information in his possession.

The buyer has the right, when it is reasonable, to require the seller
to make or obtain, pay for and hand over a statutory declaration as
to the facts (cond 4.3.2).

(c) Deducing title

A plan referred to in an abstracted deed is an integral part of the
deed and the seller must supply a copy of it at his own expense

(*Llewellyn v Earl of Jersey* (1843) 11 M & W 183). This is subject to the qualification that the plan must be necessary for properly identifying the property or correctly interpreting the deed. The Council of the Law Society decided that a purchase at auction of 20 acres of land, which the seller had purchased as part of an estate of 275 acres, was only entitled to a copy of that part of the original conveyance plan which related to the land he had bought (*Law Society's Digest*, vol 1, Opn 84, 1900).

The extent of registered land is briefly defined on the register, with a reference to the filed plan. Both the verbal description and the plan are therefore needed to determine the boundaries of the property (subject always to the general boundaries rule: pp 23–4). A buyer is always entitled to require the seller to furnish a copy of the subsisting entries on the register and of the filed plan, whatever the contract says (Land Registration Act 1925, s 110(1)). Unless the contract otherwise provides, the buyer pays for the copies when the purchase price exceeds £1,000. The Council of the Law Society recommends, as a matter of good conveyancing practice, that the copy supplied should be office copies rather than plain copies (*Law Society's Digest*, vol 1, 4th cum supp, Opn 316(i), 1968). *The Standard Conditions of Sale*, 3rd edn, place a duty on the seller to provide office copies (cond 4.2.1).

(d) Not enough land

When the examination of title discloses that the seller is not in a position to sell all the land which he has contracted to, the buyer's remedies will depend on the terms of the contract. Under an open contract, or in the absence of express conditions of sale referring to the matter, the buyer is entitled to rescind if the extent of the property differs substantially from that contracted to be sold. Where the boundary is only slightly different, the purchaser's only remedy is compensation. This must be claimed before completion, otherwise he is taken to have waived his rights.

A deficiency in area of 40 per cent justifies rescission (*Watson v Burton* [1957] 1 WLR 19). Where a property was described as including a wall and tradesman's entrance, but actually excluded the wall and gave no indefeasible right to use the entrance, the right also arose (*Brewer v Brown* (1884) 28 Ch D 309). Even though the purchaser is entitled to rescind, he may nevertheless insist on taking a conveyance at a reduced price, the compensation being assessed at a fair figure, not a penal one.

The Standard Conditions of Sale, 3rd edn, cond 7.1, contain provisions with the object of eliminating claims for compensation where discrepancies are immaterial, and restricting the buyer's rights to compensation rather than rescission in more substantial cases. Whether the right to rescind is successfully excluded in any particular case depends on whether the condition satisfies the test of reasonableness (Misrepresentation Act 1967, s 3; Unfair Contract Terms Act 1977, ss 8(1), 11(1)).

3 Conveyance

(a) Unregistered land

The buyer is entitled to have the land conveyed to him by a modern description. This need not be the description by which it was conveyed to the seller (*Re Sansom and Narbeth's Contract* [1910] 1 Ch 741), nor need it be identical to the contract description. The buyer can insist on the inclusion of measurements, even when there was none in the contract description of the property, if this will avoid litigation which would be likely without them (*Monighetti v Wandsworth Borough Council* (1908) 73 JP 91).

On the other hand, the buyer can require that the contract description is repeated in the conveyance, if the alternative would be to exclude part of the land he contracted to buy (*Lloyd v Stanbury* [1971] 1 WLR 535).

A buyer can generally insist on the conveyance referring to a plan if the verbal description is not adequate. When the words give a sufficient and satisfactory identification of the land sold, fixing all its boundaries, no plan is necessary (*Re Sharman's Contract* [1936] 1 Ch 755). A whole island off the coast was satisfactorily described by naming it and referring to two other islands by name, and without referring to a plan showing an outline and measurements (*Collector of Land Revenue, Singapore v Hoalim* [1978] AC 525).

If the verbal description is not adequate, the buyer is entitled to a plan. That plan must be to an adequate scale (*Scarfe v Adams* [1981] 1 All ER 843). For a house, a scale of 1:1250 will generally suffice (*R v Secretary of State for the Environment, ex parte Norwich City Council* [1982] QB 808). The only exception is where a plan would be particularly complicated and might itself induce litigation. The duty to provide a plan applies even if the contract did not refer to one. Even though the contract plan was stated to be for reference only and without any guarantee of accuracy, the buyer can insist on its being used without those qualifications, if the plan is required to complete a satisfactory definition of the property conveyed (*Re Sparrow and James' Contract* [1910] 2 Ch 60).

(b) Registered land

Although the same principles apply to describing the land comprised in a registered transfer as apply in the case of a conveyance of unregistered land, problems are necessarily much rarer. When the whole of the land registered under a particular title is transferred, a reference to that registration is all that is needed. In the occasional case in which part of the land has passed to a third party who has acquired a squatter's title, or the title to extra land has been acquired, the buyer would be entitled to have the property transferred by reference to a modern description, with a revised plan if necessary.

On the transfer of part of the land comprised in a title, the rules require a reference to a plan, unless the extent of the land can be clearly defined by a verbal reference to the filed plan or the general map (Land Registration Rules 1925, r 79). A transfer plan must be signed by the seller and by or on behalf of the buyer. The same thing applies to a transfer of mines and minerals separately from the surface of the land, or one of the surface without the mines and minerals, and to a transfer, grant or lease of an easement defining the dominant or servient tenement (r 113).

Chapter 3

Boundary Disputes

1 Types of action

(a) General

In default of agreement to submit them to arbitration, boundary disputes can be brought before the courts for determination in a number of ways. If the position of the boundary is the only question in issue a declaration may be sought.

An action for a declaration may be brought in the High Court under RSC Ord 15, r 16, without asking for any other relief. This jurisdiction is discretionary. There must be nothing to disentitle the plaintiff to relief, and the defendant must previously have asserted some right or formulated some specific claim. The court will not usually entertain an action where the subject matter is under £10 in value (*Westbury-on-Severn Rural Sanitary Authority v Meredith* (1885) 30 Ch D 387). Where the question in issue is the interpretation of a deed, will or other document, which may well be the case in a boundary dispute, any person interested may apply for a declaration of the rights of all the persons interested by originating summons under RSC Ord 15, r 13. The application in boundary disputes, as matters of title, will be to the Chancery Division using the *inter partes* form of originating summons: see RSC Ord 7, r 2.

An application for a declaration is usually linked with some other form of action, even in the High Court. The appropriate form where one party alleges infringement of his boundary and occupation of part of his land by the other is trespass. It is nuisance where the infringement consists of allowing such things as tree roots to spread past his boundary. The exact position of a boundary may be important in other actions too, for example under the rule in *Rylands v Fletcher* (1868) LR 3 HL 330, straying animals, contract and recovery of road charges.

An action for damages may be appropriate, where the violation of a boundary has deprived the plaintiff of the use of some of his land. Particulars of special damage must be given (*Ilkiw v Samuels* [1963] 1 WLR 991). A claim for damages can be small provided it is genuine (*Hatt & Co (Bath) Ltd v Pearce* [1978] 1 WLR 885).

Boundary disputes may, by an agreement made either at the time of the difference or before, be referred to arbitration, when the Arbitration Acts will apply.

An owner objecting to an encroachment onto his property, as where his neighbouring builds across the boundary without authority, has the common law right of self-redress against the trespasser. The intrusion can be removed. However, that right should not be exercised where the consequences are disproportionate, and it ceases when court action has been determined (*Burton v Winters* [1993] 1 WLR 1077).

(b) Registered land

Where the title to land of which the boundary is in dispute is registered, application may be made by one party to the Registrar for rectification of the register. In default of agreement, rectification may be ordered in cases of fraud, error or mistake (Land Registration Act 1925, s 82). This would cover, for instance, misinterpretation of deeds when the title was investigated for first registration. Where, however, a strip of land is, by a mistake, conveyed twice and the second purchaser registered as proprietor of it, justice may prevent rectification to adjust the boundary once the registered land has changed hands again (*Epps v Esso Petroleum Co Ltd* [1973] 1 WLR 1071).

The application is made in writing: there is no prescribed form. There is a hearing before the Solicitor to the Land Registry if the matter is not settled. Appeal against his order is by notice of motion to the Chancery Division under RSC Ord 93, r 10, and is heard by a single judge whose decision is final unless leave to appeal is granted either by him or the Court of Appeal. Notice of any appeal should be given to the Registrar as soon as possible, so that a notice of it may be entered on the register to warn purchasers.

This form of proceedings is not, however, completely satisfactory for settling disputes as it may not provide a final determination of the issues between the parties. For instance, it seems that the Solicitor (and the court on appeal from him) may construe a title deed to decide its effect upon the entries on the register, but it will still be open to the court to construe the same deed in a different sense in subsequent proceedings between the same parties where more evidence is available (*Re Dances Way, West Town, Hayling Island* [1962] Ch 490). Disputes affecting registered land may be brought before the courts in the usual way. Should the boundary be found to be different from that shown on the register, the court may order the Land Registry to effect the necessary rectification.

2 Evidence of the position of boundaries

The primary evidence available in boundary disputes is the title deeds to the properties. Extrinsic evidence is not available to vary a clear description given in a deed, but it may be called to lay before the court the information that the parties had at the time of the execution of the deed. It is also admissible in cases of ambiguity, even if only latent, ie only apparent when the deed is read by a person with knowledge of the facts. Evidence can be called to show the boundaries of the land as used prior to the grant, to prove what was meant to have been conveyed.

Evidence of reputation is only admissible where matters of general or public interest are concerned (*Evans v Merthyr Tydfil Urban Council* [1890] 1 Ch 241; *Mercer v Denne* [1905] 2 Ch 538). This would include boundaries of towns and parishes, and would only be of use in private boundary disputes where the extent of the land is defined by reference to such public boundaries. When admissible, such evidence may be oral or documentary. It may also consist of the verdict of a jury in a previous action between different parties (*Evans v Rees* (1839) 10 Ad & El 151).

(a) Civil Evidence Act 1995

The provisions of this Act are expected to be brought into force shortly. They will replace those of the Civil Evidence Act 1968 dealing with the admission of documents into evidence.

A statement in a document which is admissible evidence (hearsay is no longer excluded: s 1(1)) may be proved by producing the document or an authenticated copy of all or part of it (s 8).

(b) Business and public records

A document forming part of the records of a business or a public authority may be received in evidence without further proof (Civil Evidence Act 1995, s 9(1), yet to be brought into force).

(c) Public documents

The common law rules concerning the use of public documents as evidence have been preserved, notwithstanding the enactment of the new statute (Civil Evidence Act 1995, s 7(2)(*b*)).

The contents of public documents may generally be proved as evidence of the facts in them. Examples of such documents that have been received in evidence to prove boundaries include Domesday Book (being a record of a public survey) (*Alcock v Cooke* (1829) 5 Bing 340; *Duke of Beaufort v John Aird & Co* (1904) 20 TLR 602); a survey made under a statutory duty, eg a tithe map and tithe apportionment survey (*Knight v David* [1971] 1 WLR 1671); evidence of a tithe map was adduced in the Court of Appeal (*Minting v Ramage* [1991] EGCS 12); an ancient survey of Crown lands (*Doe d William IV v Roberts* (1844) 13 M & W 520); and a map drawn by authority of a royal commission (*New Romney Corporation v New Romney Sewers Commissioners* [1892] 1 QB 840). The survey must normally have been made with the intention that it should be available for public inspection, and the person undertaking it must be a public officer with a quasi-judicial duty to inquire into the matters recorded. It should be produced from proper custody.

A planning permission has been held to be a relevant public document (*Scott v Martin* [1987] 1 WLR 841). A consent with a plan could be referred to as evidence of the background facts against which a conveyance should be construed (*Stock v David Wilson (Homes) Anglia Ltd* [1993] CLY 527).

Surveys not intended for public inspection, or made under private auspices, are not available as public documents. This includes Crown surveys made for private or temporary purposes such as a survey by the Augmentation Office for the Crown as a private owner (*Phillips v Hudson* (1867) 2 Ch App 243), and a seventeenth century survey of coastal castles to consider whether repairs were necessary (*Mercer v Denne* [1905] 2 Ch 538). Such documents may, however, be admissible on other grounds: see (i) *Declarations of deceased persons*, p 40.

(d) Ancient documents

Ancient documents produced from proper custody which on the face of them deal with questions of ownership may be admitted in evidence to prove boundaries. Examples are leases, or documents showing that a person in occupation successfully protected his right to possession. There is a presumption relating to such documents produced from proper custody which are over 20 years old, in favour of their validity: erasures and interlineations are presumed to have been made before execution. This includes documents in the keeping of a person to whom they came in the natural course.

(e) Title deeds

The title deeds of the properties divided by a disputed boundary will be most important as evidence, and in an action a party is entitled to discovery of deeds in the other party's possession which either contain evidence of the joint title, or tend to substantiate the case of the party seeking discovery. A party may resist discovery in boundary cases only if the deeds relate exclusively to the case of the party resisting or are immaterial (which is unlikely in this type of case). Even then, a person who has been responsible for confusing the boundaries cannot resist discovery. In disputes between landlord and tenant, when the tenant has confused his own land with that demised to him, the tenant must produce his own title deeds to the landlord. The former rule that a third party called as a witness was entitled to refuse to produce his title deeds, unless he or his predecessor in title had given an acknowledgment for production to the party calling him, or his predecessor in title, no longer applies (Civil Evidence Act 1968, s 16(1)(b)).

(f) Ecclesiastical terriers

An ecclesiastical terrier is a schedule of the temporal possessions of a parish church. They are made from time to time. If produced from proper custody, they are admissible in evidence, and may be of use in proving the boundaries of glebe or adjoining lands. Proper custody would be the diocesan record office, the bishop's or the archdeacon's registry or the chest of the parish church.

(g) Ordnance Survey

Authority to carry out a complete survey of Britain and publish maps was first conferred by the Ordnance Survey Act 1841. The powers are now exercised by the Secretary of State for the Environment. Section 12 of the Act expressly provided that the powers conferred did not extend to ascertaining or altering private boundaries, and that private titles should remain unaffected. As such, the

Ordnance Survey is not therefore of evidential value. It may, however, be adopted in private deeds, and often is, in which case it is deemed to be incorporated in them and must be referred to. Many superseded Ordnance Survey maps are available as film or paper copies through Special Products, Ordnance Survey, Romsey Road, Southampton SO9 4DH, who will provide cost estimates for research and copying services. Some maps are kept in county record offices. Most are available in the Map Room of the British Library, and copies may be obtained, subject to paying a fee which will include any copyright payment.

The Ordnance Survey will prepare, for production in court, an authoritative statement on questions arising from an ordnance map. They will also nominate an expert witness to give evidence about Ordnance Survey mapping practices. A charge is made, which varies according to the time spent and expenses incurred. It is likely to exceed £50.

(h) Other maps

Private boundaries may not be proved by maps attached to inclosure awards, which, although they may prove a road to be a highway, do not conclusively delineate its boundaries.

A map drawn, accepted or acted upon by a party to the proceedings or his predecessor in title, might be available as an admission of the facts shown, though not admissible as a public document. General maps and atlases may be adduced as evidence of facts within public knowledge.

It is unlikely that Land Registry plans would be used in evidence (except where the entries on them are directly in issue) because the boundaries shown are not normally precise. If it is desired to produce any plan filed in the Registry, an office copy is admissible to the same extent as the original (Land Registration Act 1925, s 113).

(i) Declarations of deceased persons

In three cases relevant to boundary disputes the declarations of persons since deceased may be admitted in evidence: when against his pecuniary or proprietary interests; when made in the course of duty (*Price v Earl of Torrington* (1703) 1 Salk 285); and when as to public rights. In the first case the declaration must have been against the declarer's interests at that time, and have been so to his knowledge. To be admissible as made in the course of duty, the statement must concern his normal business, and be made in its normal course at or about the time to which it relates. This includes not only statements of a man holding permanent office, but also a professional man (eg a surveyor) employed on an *ad hoc* basis for the particular job concerned (*Mellor v Walmesley* [1905] 2 Ch 164). It is necessary for it to be apparent from the document that it was recorded as personal knowledge (not hearsay) and contemporaneously (*Mercer v Denne* [1905] 2 Ch 538). Declarations as to public rights must have been made before any controversy arose. They must concern rights exercisable by the whole community (such as public rights of way) or a substantial part of it (such as a right of common), and such declarations must directly assert or deny the existence of the rights.

The effect of these provisions is to admit some documents that would otherwise be excluded. For example, surveys of Crown property made for the Crown's private purposes do not come within the definition of public documents for the purposes of admissibility, but if of some antiquity (so that the death of the author can be presumed without further proof, by reason of the normal life span) they will be available as evidence, by virtue of being a declaration made by a deceased person in the course of his duty.

(j) Acts of ownership

Evidence may be given of acts of ownership of property to establish boundaries. Acts which have been admitted include tree planting and felling, cutting grass, grazing cattle, fishing, turning off strangers or preventing them from removing soil. The perambulation of his boundaries by the lord of the manor is evidence of the extent of his manor.

If the dispute concerns the ownership of an existing boundary feature, or the question is whether the boundary is down one side or the other of it or down the middle, evidence of acts of ownership exercised over the feature is admissible. Such acts are clipping and trimming a hedge, repairing a fence or wall, or clearing a ditch.

Acts of ownership are not conclusive evidence, particularly if they are relatively slight and for the convenience of the person doing them. He might not have been under a legal obligation, or even have had the right, to do them. Acts carried out without the contesting neighbour's knowledge, and therefore without his acquiescence, are not good evidence (*Henniker v Howard* (1904) 90 LT 157).

(k) Mode of construction of boundary features

It is customary to build brick walls and close-boarded fences so that the piers and upright supports protrude onto the land of the owner of the wall or fence. This is so that the wall or fence may go right up to the boundary; if the protrusions were to project into the neighbour's property they would constitute a trespass which the owner could be made to remove. (Nevertheless, the foundations of party walls can project in certain cases: see pp 52–3.) Accordingly, the mode of construction of this type of wall or fence is *prima facie* evidence of its ownership. But it is not conclusive, because owners are not compelled to build in this way: they may set the wall or fence back very slightly to avoid trespassing. A fence reversing the usual method of construction has the advantage that repairs can be carried out from the owner's side.

(l) Local custom

Occasionally local custom may help to establish the position of a boundary. For example, in one case it was alleged, but not established, that private properties which adjoined a common were always considered to extend four feet on the common side of their hedges so that a fence could be erected to protect the hedge from animals grazing on the common (*Collis v Amphlett* [1918] 1 Ch 232; [1920] AC 271).

3 Seller and buyer

Under an open contract, or in the absence of express conditions of sale referring to this question, the buyer is entitled to rescind if the property differs substantially from that contracted to be sold. Where the boundary is only slightly different, the buyer's only right is compensation. This must be claimed before completion, otherwise the buyer is taken to have waived his rights. A deficiency in area of 40 per cent justifies rescission (*Watson v Burton* [1957] 1 WLR 19), and where a property is described as including a wall and tradesmen's entrance, but excludes the wall and gives no indefeasible right to use the entrance, the right also arises (*Brewer v Brown* (1884) 28 Ch D 309). Even though the purchaser is entitled to rescind, he may nevertheless insist on taking a conveyance at a reduced purchase price, the compensation being assessed at a fair figure, not a penal one.

Provision is made as to this in *Standard Conditions of Sale*, 3rd edn, cond 7.1.3, with the object of restricting the parties' rights to compensation rather than rescission, except in cases of substantial discrepancies. The extent to which the right to rescind is successfully restricted depends on whether the condition satisfies the reasonableness test (Misrepresentation Act 1967, s 3; Unfair Contract Terms Act 1977, ss 8(1), 11(1)).

4 Landlord and tenant

A tenant who impugns his landlord's title gives the landlord grounds for forfeiture of his lease, so boundary disputes, which are normally disputes as to title, are rare between landlord and tenant.

The relationship of landlord and tenant imposes an obligation upon the tenant to preserve the boundaries of the demised premises, and to prevent their being destroyed so that the landlord's property cannot be delimited (*Attorney-General v Fullerton* (1813) 2 Ves & B 263). Where the tenant has confused the boundaries by merging adjoining premises, the landlord may apply to the court to have the boundary ascertained, even during the term of the demise (*Spike v Harding* (1878) 7 Ch D 871). To give jurisdiction, the plaintiff must show by evidence, or the defendant's admission, that he has legal title to the land, that the boundaries are confused and that the tenant is in possession of part at least. The application is to the Chancery Division and the practice is to direct an enquiry in chambers to ascertain the boundary. If at the end of the term of a lease the boundaries are so confused that the tenant cannot render up precisely the landlord's property, he is bound to restore land of equal value. This is ascertained as fairly as may be, but doubts are resolved against the tenant, because he is at fault.

5 Crown lands

Formerly, special provisions applied to the settlement of disputes relating to Crown lands, and arbitration awards had to be enrolled in the Office of Land Revenue Records and Enrolments (now housed with and superseded by the Public Record Office, Chancery Lane, London WC2A 1LR). These provisions were repealed by the Crown Estates Act 1961. In all Crown leases there is now inserted a provision for the Crown Estate Commissioners to settle boundary disputes. The address of the Commissioners is Crown Estate Office, 13–15 Carlton House Terrace, London SW1Y 5AH.

6 Duchy of Cornwall lands

The Duke of Cornwall (or, during his minority, the Sovereign or other person appointed by her, on his behalf), with the previous consent of the Treasury, may make any arrangement to settle a boundary dispute affecting Duchy lands. The agreement must be enrolled in the Office of the Duchy of Cornwall, after which it is conclusive and binding on the Duke of Cornwall and all other interested parties. In the case of dispute as to the terms of such an agreement, the Duke of Cornwall may, with Treasury consent, agree to refer the matter to arbitration. The award must be enrolled in the Duchy Office, when it will be binding.

Enrolment is effected at the Duchy Office which is at 10 Buckingham Gate, London SW1E 6LA, to which documents may be sent by post. Enrolment must be within six months of the date of the document, but enrolments out of time made *nunc pro tunc* may be permitted on reasonable cause being shown. A certificate of enrolment is admissible in all courts as proof of the original instrument and its enrolment.

Chapter 4

Party Walls

1 What is a party wall?

For the purposes of the Party Wall etc Act 1996 a 'party wall' is a wall separating buildings in different ownership or the wall of a building standing partly on the land of one owner and partly on the land of another. A 'party fence wall' stands on lands in different ownership but is not part of a building (s 20). These definitions are dealt with below (p 49).

The 1996 Act aside, the term 'party wall' is now applied to walls dividing properties in different ownership in three situations: first, where the wall is divided vertically in half, each neighbour owning the half on his side; secondly, where the wall is entirely the property of one adjoining owner, but is subject to easements or rights in favour of the other to have it maintained dividing the properties; thirdly, and most common, where the wall is divided vertically, but each part is subject to cross-easements in favour of the other. These different situations will be examined separately below. Before 1926 party walls were often held by the adjoining owners as tenants in common, but in abolishing this form of joint ownership at law, the LPA 1925 substituted a division of the wall with cross-easements.

(a) Vertically divided walls

A boundary wall which is built so that its centre exactly follows the dividing line will fall into this first class, being divided vertically into halves each owned by the landowner adjoining it (*Matts v Hawkins* (1813) 5 Taunt 20). Even though it may be built at the joint expense of the neighbours it is not subject to joint ownership. Whether the wall is built exactly astride the boundary is a question of fact, but minor inaccuracies will be ignored (*Reading v Barnard* (1827) Mood & M 71).

(b) Walls in single ownership

Where a boundary wall is built exclusively on the land of one owner it belongs to him in the absence of agreement to the contrary. The adjoining owner may acquire rights over it by agreement or prescription. (An easement of support may be acquired under the Prescription Act 1832 by user as of right for 20 years, provided that the owner of the servient tenement has not during the period been under a disability, or 40 years notwithstanding such disability.) Long use of a wall as part of a building on his land does not give the adjoining owner title to the wall (as it will not normally amount to exclusive possession of it adverse to the owner), but may give him an easement of support for his roof (*Waddington v Naylor* (1889) 60 LT 480). Acquisition of a wall by adverse possession can be avoided by fixing a notice to it visible to the public stating to whom it belongs.

(c) Divided walls subject to cross-easements

Walls expressly made subject to a tenancy in common, or since 1925 to the LPA 1925, s 38, or other walls not exclusively on one person's property (and not within the first class above), come within this class. In cases of doubt before 1926, there was a presumption that a tenancy in common existed. This applied, for instance, when the circumstances of building the wall and how much land each adjoining owner contributed were not known (*Cubitt v Porter* (1828) 8 B & C 257). Similarly, where both parties used the wall, this was sufficient *prima facie* evidence for the presumption to operate (ibid).

Since 1925, cases where previously a tenancy in common existed or would have been created, and walls which are or are expressed to be party walls, are covered by the LPA 1925, s 38. This provides that they shall be regarded as severed vertically, each part enjoying such rights of support and user over the other as would have subsisted if a valid tenancy in common of it had existed. These rights vary according to the circumstances, but normally extend to permitting the use of the wall by either adjoining owner for any purpose contemplated when the grant of the wall was made (eg support of a roof) without interference. A person interested in a party structure affected by the section may apply to the court for a declaration of the rights and interests of those interested, when the court may make such order as it thinks fit (LPA 1925, s 38(2)). Although the section refers to 'walls or structures', its provision for dividing them vertically prevents it applying to ceilings and floors between flats and maisonettes in separate ownership.

2 Repairing party walls: overview

The repair obligations relating to a particular party wall may be governed by a contract between the parties in question or may arise under a lease. That aside, the right of one owner to repair a wall, which is not exclusively his, may arise under various provisions.

The Law of Property Act 1925, s 38, does not directly confer such rights. It in effect declares that cross-easements exist, and those easements confer rights at common law. The Access to Neighbouring Land Act 1992 (pp 86–95) offers a property owner who needs access to neighbouring property to do repairs the chance to obtain a county court order to authorise it. This applies to party wall repairs (*Dean v Walker* [1996] NPC 78). Finally, the Party Wall etc Act 1996 gives a property owner the right to repair a party wall p 51.

The provisions applying to repairs in each of these three cases differ, and so do their consequences. It is also necessary to distinguish the separate authority to carry out new work which only the 1996 Act gives.

The position may be summarised in this way:

3 Party Wall etc Act 1996

(a) Commencement date

The Act comes into force on a day to be appointed by the Secretary of State (s 22(2)). When this book went to press, no commencement order had been made and no date had been announced. It seemed likely that the Act would be brought into force on or after 1 April 1997.

(b) Origin

The 1996 Act effectively extends to the whole country rules which have for many years applied in central London (London Buildings Acts (Amendment) Act 1939). This local legislation is to be repealed when the general Act comes into force (1996 Act, s 21(1)). Although there are some amendments to the London Act,

FIGURE 4.1

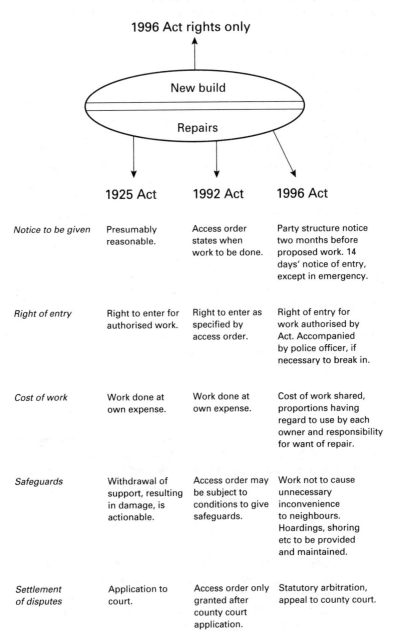

1996 Act rights only

New build

Repairs

1925 Act   1992 Act   1996 Act

	1925 Act	1992 Act	1996 Act
Notice to be given	Presumably reasonable.	Access order states when work to be done.	Party structure notice two months before proposed work. 14 days' notice of entry, except in emergency.
Right of entry	Right to enter for authorised work.	Right to enter as specified by access order.	Right of entry for work authorised by Act. Accompanied by police officer, if necessary to break in.
Cost of work	Work done at own expense.	Work done at own expense.	Cost of work shared, proportions having regard to use by each owner and responsibility for want of repair.
Safeguards	Withdrawal of support, resulting in damage, is actionable.	Access order may be subject to conditions to give safeguards.	Work not to cause unnecessary inconvenience to neighbours. Hoardings, shoring etc to be provided and maintained.
Settlement of disputes	Application to court.	Access order only granted after county court application.	Statutory arbitration, appeal to county court.

many of the provisions remain the same. Accordingly, court decisions interpreting that Act should equally apply to the new one.

(c) Scheme of the Act

The aim of the 1996 Act is to maximise the use of property, while protecting adjoining owners. To this end, it gives property owners three sets of rights relating to walls on their boundaries and sometimes to floors which constitute the boundaries of their property. First, they have rights of repair; secondly, they may extend the use they make of the wall and do consequential construction work; thirdly, they can erect new walls on or over their boundaries. There are also restrictive provisions: an owner who wants to excavate on his own land may have to give prior notice to his neighbour in circumstances where the excavation might prejudice a structure on the neighbouring land.

Before exercising a statutory right an owner has to serve notice on the adjoining owner specifying what is proposed, and the adjoining owner has the right to challenge it by serving a counter-notice. This gives him the chance to suggest modifications to the proposed works, so that they are more useful to him. There are provisions for dispute resolution, and a subsequent appeal to the courts, if they disagree.

(d) Scope of the Act

The 1996 Act defines a number of the terms it uses. The definitions are important, because they explain the circumstances which the Act covers.

The term 'party wall' covers two cases. First, it is a wall, forming part of a building, which stands on lands in different ownership. This ignores a case where the overlap is merely the extent of artificial supports on which the wall rests. Secondly, it is that part of a wall which separates buildings in different ownership. This contrasts with a 'party fence wall', which is a boundary wall that does not form part of a building. It must be used to separate the adjoining properties, or have been constructed for that purpose. It straddles the boundary, which means standing on lands in different ownership, to a greater extent than merely the artificial supports for the wall. A 'party structure' extends the term 'party wall' to include floor partitions and other structures separating buildings or parts of buildings approached by separate staircases or separate entrances

(1996 Act, s 20). The equivalent definition in the London Act required the separate entrances to be 'from without'. Dropping those words make it clear that the Act is not only referring to parts of buildings with an entrance to the open air.

The 1996 Act uses 'owner' in a broad sense. There are three categories. It includes (1996 Act, s 20):

(*a*) a person in receipt of the whole or part of the rents and profits of the property. This includes a long leaseholder, even though he has sublet for a term longer than from year to year (*Hunt v Harris* (1865) 19 CB(NS) 13);

(*b*) a person in possession of the land, but not as a mortgagee or as a tenant from year to year or a lesser term or a tenant at will;

(*c*) a contracting buyer or tenant, except under an agreement for a tenancy from year to year or for a lesser term.

This means that there may be more than one 'owner' of a particular piece of land. Say, eg, that *A* owns the freehold, previously let it to *B* for 99 years, who in turn sublet to *C* for 25 years, and *A* now contracts to sell the freehold to *D* subject to the leases: all four qualify as 'owner'.

A 'building owner' is a landowner who wants to exercise statutory rights. He may own open land, rather than a building. All (or both) the owners of jointly owned property constitute the building owner: so, to be valid, a statutory notice must be given by all of them (*Lehmann v Herman* [1993] 1 EGLR 172). The same must apply to the 'adjoining owner', but the difficulty of not knowing who owns premises can be overcome when serving a notice by addressing it to 'the owner' of named premises (1996 Act, s 15(2)(*a*)).

The 1996 Act does apply to Crown land (s 19).

The only property to which the 1996 Act does not apply is land belonging to one of the Inns of Court in inner London (s 18), ie the boroughs of Camden, Greenwich, Hackney, Hammersmith, Islington, Kensington and Chelsea, Lambeth, Lewisham, Southwark, Tower Hamlets, Wandsworth and Westminster (London Government Act 1963, s 43).

(*e*) *What an owner may do: existing structures*

Where the boundary of adjoining properties in different ownership is built over, or there is a party fence wall or the external wall of a building on the boundary, the 1996 Act gives the owners extensive rights to do work on the existing structures (1996 Act, s 2). To exercise the rights he must follow the statutory procedure (p 52) or have the adjoining owner's or occupier's written consent to his serving notices on the adjoining owner.

The work the owner may do is as follows (s 2). The authority is generally subject to an obligation to make good all damage to premises, internal furnishings and decorations, and in appropriate cases to raising flues and chimney stacks.

(*a*) Underpinning, thickening or raising a party structure or party fence wall, or his own external wall built against one of them. If the work is necessary because of a defect or want of repair, the duty to make good does not apply. The cost is then shared in proportions reflecting responsibility for the defect or lack of repair and the use each owner makes of the wall or structure (s 11(4)).

(*b*) Making good, repairing, or demolishing and rebuilding a party structure or party fence wall which is defective or in need of repair.

(*c*) Exposing a party wall or party structure previously enclosed. Adequate weathering must be provided.

(*d*) Raising, lowering or rebuilding a party fence wall, including doing so to use it as a party wall. If the adjoining owner only uses it as a boundary wall, he can be called upon to contribute to the cost of requiring it to be more than two metres high (s 11(7)).

(*e*) Where a partition separates buildings in different ownership but does not comply with statutory requirements, demolishing the partition and replacing it with a party wall which does comply. Buildings connected by arches or other structures over a public way or someone else's passage may similarly be demolished and replaced if they do not comply with statutory requirements. A building and structure erected before 18 July 1996 (the day the Act was passed) is deemed to comply with statutory requirements if it complied when it was erected.

(*f*) Demolishing a party structure which is not strong or high enough for a proposed new building, and replacing it with one which is. The replacement need not be so high or thick, provided it serves the adjoining owner's purpose.

(*g*) Cutting into a party structure for any purpose (including inserting a damp proof course) or into the adjoining owner's wall to insert flashing or other weather proofing of another wall built against it.

(*h*) Cutting away projections to allow the building or under-pinning of a party, party fence, external or boundary wall, or to enable the building owner to build a vertical wall against the adjoining owner's wall or building.

Procedure

A building owner wishing to exercise any of these rights must serve a 'party structure notice' on the adjoining owner at least two months before work is to begin. This specifies the nature and details of the work proposed. Where there are to be foundations reinforced with steel rods or beams ('special foundations'), plans must also be served. The notice ceases to have effect if the work is not started within 12 months after it is served and prosecuted with diligence (s 3).

The adjoining owner has one month within which to serve a counter-notice. In the case of special foundations, the counter-notice may require them to be stronger and/or deeper to accommodate a new building for the adjoining owner. In other cases it may require the building of chimneys, flues, copings, piers or recesses for the adjoining owner's convenience. Plans of the works specified must accompany the notice.

The building owner must comply with the requirements of the counter-notice, unless they would be injurious to him, cause him unnecessary inconvenience, or unnecessarily delay the work (s 4).

(f) What an owner may do: new structures

The owner of land on one side of a boundary which is not built on, or where there is merely a boundary wall which is neither a party fence wall nor the external wall of a building, may build up to or straddling the boundary on following the statutory procedure (1996 Act, s 1).

An owner who wants to build a party wall or a party fence wall, extending across the boundary, must give at least one month's notice with details of his proposal. Only if the adjoining owner agrees (by serving notice within 14 days), can the wall be a party wall or a party fence wall. It is built half on the land of each owner, or in a different position which they agree, and the expense is shared in proportions having regard to each owner's use of the wall and the cost of labour and materials when they use it. If the adjoining owner does not agree to the wall being built across the boundary, the building owner must erect it wholly on his own land, at his own expense.

Even if a building owner proposes to build a wall on the boundary, but wholly on his own land, he must serve notice at least one month before work starts, describing the intended wall.

An owner building a boundary wall wholly on his own land—whether from choice or because the adjoining owner did not agree to a party wall or a party fence wall—may put projecting footings and foundations into the adjoining land during the year after he gave his notice. He must also compensate any adjoining owner or occupier for damage caused by building the wall and from making footings and foundations.

The requirements of the Act are mandatory. An interlocutory order, to remove new building work over the boundary line, was made against defendants who were aware of the equivalent procedure under the former London Building Acts, but did not follow it (*London & Manchester Assurance Co Ltd v O&H Construction Ltd* [1989] 2 EGLR 185).

(g) *Relationship to other obligations*

A land owner may have other obligations which appear to run contrary to some of the rights given by the 1996 Act. For example, a restrictive covenant or a tenant's covenant in a lease may forbid any alteration to a boundary wall. The wording used by the Act in relation to existing structures, 'A building owner shall have the following rights' (s 2(2)) suggests that, assuming the statutory procedure is followed, it overrides a private prohibition.

However, the Act operates to regulate the relations between the neighbouring owners or occupiers. Accordingly, although it may well govern relations between them, it would presumably not override bargains between a landowner and someone other than the neighbouring landowner. A landlord might or might not own or occupy adjoining land, and therefore the effect of the Act on a lease will vary. Further the Act would presumably have no effect on other forms of regulation, eg conditions attached to a planning permission.

(h) *Excavation*

The Act is not confined to building work at the boundary between properties in separate ownership. A building owner who excavates within three metres, and sometimes six metres, of a structure on adjoining land to below the level of that structure's foundations, may be called upon to underpin the structure or strengthen the foundations (1996 Act, s 6).

(i) Execution and cost of works

A building owner must not exercise his statutory rights in a way, or at a time, which unnecessarily inconveniences any adjoining owner or occupier. If any part of the adjoining land or building is laid open, the building owner must maintain and pay for a proper hoarding or shoring as necessary to protect the property and for the security of the occupier (1996 Act, s 7). An adjoining owner may require the building owner to give security before starting work (s 12).

The building owner has a right to enter land and premises to do the work, as do his servants, agents and workmen, and to obstruct them is an offence (s 16). They must give 14 days' notice except in an emergency. They may stay during normal working hours, and may remove furniture and fittings and take other necessary action. In order to enter, they may break open fences and doors if accompanied by a police officer (s 8).

The cost of authorised work is borne by the building owner, except where the Act provides for its being shared (s 11(1)).

(j) Disputes

There is a statutory procedure for settling all disputes between adjoining owners (1996 Act, s 10). Either they agree to appoint one surveyor ('agreed surveyor'), or each appoints his own and the two surveyors appoint a third, the three acting together. Appointments are made in writing and are irrevocable. There are provisions to cover cases where a party fails to appoint a surveyor or the surveyor fails to act or becomes incapable or dies. A surveyor appointed under this procedure has a right of entry to the premises during normal working hours (s 8(5)), and it is an offence to obstruct him (s 16).

For this purpose 'surveyor' is anyone, other than a party, appointed to determine a dispute (s 20). The definition is therefore circular, but it certainly does not require any professional qualification.

The award to settle the dispute may determine what work may be done, how and when. It may also settle incidental matters and order the payment of reasonable costs. The award cannot settle future disputes between the parties, but it can impose continuing maintenance obligations (*Marchant v Capital & Counties plc* [1983] 2 EGLR 155). Nevertheless, the jurisdiction is limited to disputes concerning work authorised by the Act. It does not extend to related matters, eg damage caused by the collapse of a boundary wall during the period allowed for the adjoining owner to give consent to works (*Woodhouse v Consolidated Property Corporation Ltd* (1992) 66 P&CR 234).

The agreed surveyor may make the award. Where there are three surveyors, two or three of them may make the award, or either of the parties or their surveyors may call upon the third surveyor to do so.

An award is conclusive, but within 14 days of its delivery either party may appeal to the county court (procedure: CCR Ord 3, r 6). The court's powers extend to rescinding or modifying an award. For that purpose, it can receive evidence of fact or opinion, including evidence not available to the surveyor(s) (*Chartered Society of Physiotherapy v Simmonds Church Smiles* [1995] 1 EGLR 155).

(k) Successor in title

The Act leaves a series of questions, as to the effect of one of the neighbouring properties changing hands, unanswered. The rights which a building owner can establish under the Act, either to erect a new building on a boundary (s 1) or in relation to an existing party structure (s 2), are described as rights to carry out certain works. The wording is appropriate for them to be rights *in rem*, exercisable whoever owns the adjoining land (unless, presumably, it becomes land to which the Act does not apply: s 18; p 50). Accordingly, there should be no difficulty once the statutory procedure has been completed. The right is exercisable on the adjoining land, whoever owns it. Presumably also it is exercisable by the owner for the time being of the 'dominant' land, who by owning the land and desiring to do the work becomes the 'building owner'.

However, there is no express provision to bring the existence of a party wall agreement or award to the attention of later property owners. They are not registrable at the Land Registry, and as they do not relate to an owner's power of disposition there must be doubt whether a notice can properly be registered.

There may be greater difficulty if the adjoining land is transferred while the statutory procedure is still in progress. Is an incoming owner bound by notices served on or by his predecessor, or must the procedure start again? Again, there is no provision for registration to warn a buyer that something is afoot, although it is pre-contract information which the seller should divulge.

Other difficulties can arise if the building owner parts with his interest after giving security for the performance of statutory work (s 12). If his successor in title does not fully comply with his obligations can the adjoining owner have recourse to that security? Is the outgoing building owner bound to leave the security deposited? What are the rights of the former and later building owners against each other?

(*l*) Landlord and tenant

The rights of tenants may raise other queries. The Act's definition of 'owner' clearly includes a tenant for a longer term than year to year (s 20). Accordingly, a tenant for a term of years who uses the statutory procedure obtains a right to carry out the work, which is enforceable against the adjoining owner. If that adjoining owner happens to be his landlord, there is little doubt that any contrary term in the lease is overridden. But if that is not the case, there seems no reason to suppose, as there is nothing to that effect in the statute, that in dealing with the position between the tenant and his neighbour the Act negatives the effect of a lease covenant forbidding the tenant to do the work he proposes.

The position is presumably the same if the landlord who owns neighbouring property proposes to do work which he expressly covenants in the lease not to do, or which might derogate from the grant. He obtains statutory authority. However, it must be borne in mind that a landlord's covenant for quiet enjoyment protects the tenant against the lawful acts of others. That raises the question whether a landlord exercising statutory rights could nevertheless be liable for damages for breach of that covenant.

The Act defines 'adjoining owner' to mean 'any owner and any occupier' of adjoining land (s 20). Presumably, this means that the response to a building owner's statutory notice must come from all those with interests in the adjoining land. This would include both landlord and tenants, and here the use of the word 'occupier' brings in tenants with shorter terms. To ensure that they speak with the same voice, landlords may consider including in leases a covenant requiring the tenant to subscribe to any response they make. This would mirror the common lease provision which requires the tenant to join in the landlord's response to applications for planning permission relating to the development of neighbouring land.

4 Common law obligations

(a) Support

An easement of support for one part of a party wall by another in separate ownership may be acquired by grant, express or implied, or by prescription. In the absence of acquisition by any of these methods, there is no right of support (*Peyton v London Corporation* (1829) 9 B & C 725). If support is withdrawn by the adjoining owner no action lies for the resulting damage. This remains so even if the building owner has covenanted with the neighbour who withdraws the support to keep his building in repair, and the withdrawal makes it impossible to comply with his covenant (*Colebeck v The Girdlers Company* (1876) 1 QBD 234).

Cases now falling under s 38 of the LPA 1925 will have such an easement, and where part of a wall is granted by the owner to his neighbour with the intention of making it a party wall, the grant and reservation is implied of such cross-easements as are necessary to carry out the parties' intentions for the joint use of the wall (which will vary according to the facts of each case) (*Jones v Pritchard* [1908] 1 Ch 630, 635). This right binds a local authority which demolishes the servient tenement under a clearance order, even though it acts under a statutory duty, and accordingly it must provide alternative support (*Bond v Norman, Bond v Nottingham Corporation* [1940] Ch 429). Where the ownership of the wall is split vertically without mutual rights, neither half is entitled to support from the other. Rights of support exist only where houses adjoin, so the demolition of the next but one house in a terrace is not an actionable withdrawal of support (*Solomon v Vintners' Co* (1859) 5 H & N 585). Nevertheless, in cases where no easement of support exists, an action in negligence may be maintained where damage is caused by the adjoining owner's failure to observe a proper standard of care (*St Anne's Well Brewery Co v Roberts* (1928) 140 LT 1).

Where support is wrongfully withdrawn, the action will be for nuisance, see p 59. Even where damage has been suffered, the adjoining owner is not liable for merely failing to keep his building or part of the wall in repair, only for positive acts resulting in the withdrawal of support (*Sack v Jones* [1925] Ch 235). In these cases he is equally liable for the acts of independent contractors engaged by him (*Bower v Peate* (1876) 1 QBD 321). The adjoining owner who is liable continues to be so even though he may sell his property before some or all of the resulting damage becomes apparent. The occupier who succeeds him is not liable (*Hall v Duke of Norfolk* [1900] 2 Ch 493).

In the case of a boundary wall in single ownership there will be an easement for natural support, but this relates only to the support of the soil. A withdrawal of support for the wall is in such a case, therefore, only actionable if it is such as to cause a greater than minimal fall of soil, whatever the effect on the wall. In addition, there may be an easement for the support of the wall itself, acquired by grant or prescription. Such an easement is extinguished if the dominant owner alters the use of the wall in a way substantially to prejudice the enjoyment of the servient tenement (*Ray v Fairway Motors (Barnstaple) Ltd* (1969) 20 P & CR 261).

(b) Repairs

An easement of support does not cast upon the joint owner of a party wall any positive obligation to keep his part of the wall in repair. Similar duties may nevertheless arise as a result of the law of nuisance, see section (c) *Nuisance*. If a party wall collapses because of neglect by one owner, the other has no right of action (*Sack v Jones* [1925] Ch 235). The other owner need not, however, sit by and watch the wall crumble, but may enter his neighbour's property in order to carry out repairs (*Bond v Nottingham Corporation* [1940] Ch 429, 439). Where the easement is one of support only, without any additional repairing obligation, there is no right to reimbursement for the cost of repairs to someone else's wall (*The Highway Board, etc, of Macclesfield v Grant* (1882) 51 LJQB 357).

One property owner protected his building from exposure to the weather through a party wall, following the demolition of the neighbouring building, by building eaves out over the neghbour's land. He successfully resisted an application for a mandatory injunction to remove the eaves, because the court exercised its discretion taking into account the neighbour's conduct (*Tollemache & Cobbold Breweries v Reynolds* [1983] 2 EGLR 158).

An adjoining owner is entitled to make use of a party wall for the purpose originally intended. If in doing so the neighbouring property is damaged, he is not liable (*Jones v Pritchard* [1908] 1 Ch 630).

If one of the owners demolishes and rebuilds for such purposes, he is bound to see that the operations are carried out with reasonable care, skill and speed, whether he does them personally or through independent contractors (*Murly v M'Dermott* (1838) 8 Ad & El 138; *Murray v Hall* (1849) 7 CB 441). Positive action in shoring up the remaining property is not required if the wall is wholly owned by the person demolishing it (*Southwark and Vauxhall Water Co v Wandsworth Board of Works* [1898] 2 Ch 603, 612).

If a party wall to which s 38 of the LPA 1925 applies is damaged by a third party, each adjoining owner can only recover half of the cost of its repair, as each now only owns half the wall. In so far as one adjoining owner suffers a withdrawal of support for his half by damage done to the wall by the other adjoining owner's tenant, his remedy is against the owner, not the tenant, because the Act places the burden of the easement upon him (*Apostal v Simmons* [1936] 1 All ER 207).

(c) *Nuisance*

One neighbour may be liable to the other in nuisance as a result of disrepair to a party wall. This can effectively create repairing obligations where otherwise none exists. Where dry rot spread through a party wall, the owner on whose side it started was held liable in damages, because she should reasonably have appreciated the danger and there were preventative steps she could reasonably have taken (*Bradburn v Lindsay* [1983] 2 All ER 408). An action in nuisance was also successful when subsidence caused damage to a party wall, because the demolition of the house on one side caused the clay soil to dry out. The nuisance was an interference with the easement of support (*Brace v South Eastern Regional Housing Association* [1984] 1 EGLR 144).

Chapter 5

Duty to Fence

1 No general duty

A landowner is not, simply by reason of his owning property, under any obligation to fence his boundaries. There are, however, many cases where there will be such a duty, owed either to certain persons only or to the public at large. The circumstances in which the duty arises are dealt with in detail below. They fall into the following general categories: obligations imposed by agreement; arising by prescription; imposed because of the nature of the land, its situation or the use to which it is put; and special statutory obligations.

Where no obligation exists there can be no liability for damage sustained solely by reason of the lack of a fence. However, where a fence has been erected even though there is no obligation to do so, and it is in a dangerous condition, its owner may be liable for damage resulting from its condition. In appropriate circumstances an action could be maintained in nuisance (where there is detriment to a neighbour's enjoyment of his land: *Harrold v Watney* [1898] 2 QB 320), in negligence (where damage is caused to a person who must have been in the landowner's contemplation and to whom he owes a duty of care: *Terry v Ashton* (1876) 1 QBD 314), independently of these causes of action if the damage flows naturally from the defective fence (*Firth v Bowling Iron Co* (1878) 3 CPD 254), or against a landlord who has undertaken to repair (Defective Premises Act 1972, s 4).

2 Obligations on freehold owners

(a) *Covenants on conveying freeholds*

A covenant to erect and/or maintain a fence contained in a conveyance of freehold property is valid and enforceable between the parties to the conveyance, subject only to the usual limitation period of 12 years from the date of the breach of covenant for suing on a deed. There is, however, no completely satisfactory way to ensure that the obligation to fence will bind every person into whose hands the land comes. Normal conveyancing practice is for the covenantor to obtain an indemnity from his successor in title against loss suffered by him because of a future breach of the covenant, but this does not make the covenant directly enforceable against the new owner. At common law the burden of covenants never passed with the land. Equity modified this in the case of restrictive covenants (*Tulk v Moxhay* (1848) 2 Phil 774), but a covenant to fence is a positive covenant and is not therefore affected (*Jones v Price* [1965] 2 QB 618). The benefit of the equitable rules cannot be obtained by phrasing in negative form what is in effect a positive covenant.

A number of possible methods of attaching a fencing obligation to a freehold may be mentioned, although some are rather involved and therefore only likely to be employed in cases where the need is particularly pressing.

The first involves the creation of an estate rentcharge issuing out of the land on which the obligation is to be imposed. This form of rentcharge was introduced by the Rentcharges Act 1977, s 2. The amount of the rentcharge cannot exceed a nominal sum, except to the extent that it pays for maintenance or repairs to the fence. It is not subject to compulsory redemption (s 8(4)).

The covenant to fence is made one of the covenants entered into with the owner of the rentcharge. A right of re-entry may be reserved to the owner of the rent when it is created, which would be exercisable on breach of covenant, and should be an adequate sanction. The right to exercise it need not be confined to the perpetuity period (Perpetuities and Accumulations Act 1964, s 11(1)). A similar, more limited, provision means that the right does not have to be confined to the perpetuity period in a conveyance of Crown lands by the Crown Estate Commissioners (Crown Estates Act 1961, s 3(8)).

A second way to enforce a fencing covenant is to reserve a right of re-entry in favour of the owner of retained land, when selling part of a holding. A seller does not have to retain a reversion in the land sold in order to do that. The drawback is that unless any default complained of is grave and wilful, it is likely that equitable relief will be granted (*Shiloh Spinners Ltd v Harding* [1973] AC 691).

It has also been suggested that the principle of *Halsall v Brizell* [1957] Ch 169, could be employed here: anyone taking advantage of benefits granted by a deed must comply with obligations which it imposes to contribute to costs. That case related, amongst other benefits, to sea walls. Presumably, therefore, there is no difficulty in establishing that a purchaser takes the benefit of a fence or wall, even though the enjoyment of it is essentially passive. However, it is not clear whether the principle extends beyond making an obligation to pay money binding, to enforcing a positive obligation to do work.

The last possibility is, instead of conveying the freehold, for the seller to grant to the purchaser a lease for at least 300 years at a peppercorn rent and without a proviso for re-entry, so that the buyer can convert it into a fee simple by deed poll under s 153 of the LPA 1925. The obligations created by the covenants in such a lease do not come to an end when the term is enlarged into a freehold, but continue to attach to the freehold (subs (8)). Accordingly, if the covenant that was required as to fencing was inserted in the lease originally, the obligation would be imposed on successive owners of the freehold. The drawback of this method, which in any event would hardly be suitable for widespread use on the development of an estate, is that it is not clear what measure of damages (if any) would be recoverable in an action for breach of covenant. A landlord normally recovers the amount of the damage to his reversion, but here he has no reversion. It may therefore be that there is no effective sanction to support this obligation.

The Lands Tribunal has held that it has no jurisdiction to discharge a positive covenant to fence, under s 84 of the LPA 1925, because it is a purely personal covenant (*Re Blyth Corporation's Application* (1963) 14 P & CR 56 (LT)). If a covenant is satisfactorily made to bind successors in title, it is an open question whether it could be varied. The section refers to a 'restriction', and it may be that that would never be apt to include a positive covenant

Where the freehold of a property was purchased under the provisions for individual leasehold enfranchisement in the Leasehold Reform Act 1967 or collective leasehold enfranchisement under the Leasehold Reform, Housing and Urban Development Act 1993, a management scheme may apply. The terms of the scheme bind the owner of the property for the time being. They can require boundary walls to be maintained (*Mosley v Cooper* [1990] 1 EGLR 124). New schemes can be introduced, but only with the consent of the Secretary of State. Existing schemes can be varied by applying to a leasehold valuation tribunal (Leasehold Reform, Housing and Urban Development Act 1993, s 75).

(b) Damages on breach of covenant

On a failure to erect a boundary wall in accordance with a covenant to do so, the convenantee who owns the adjoining land can recover damages equal to the cost of carrying out the work on his own land. The amount of damages is not limited to the loss of value resulting from the lack of a wall, nor to the cost of erecting the cheapest possible fence in its place (*Radford v De Froberville* [1977] 1 WLR 1262). Damages which amount to the cost of the work when judgment is given, even if this is greater than it would have been at the date the work should have been done, can be recovered by a plaintiff who could not reasonably have done the work earlier (*Dodd Properties (Kent) Ltd v Canterbury City Council* [1980] 1 WLR 433).

3 Landlord and tenant

(a) Express covenants

Covenants to erect and/or maintain fences are often found in leases, and they may be by either party. This is certainly one of the matters that a lease should deal with explicitly wherever possible. If there is a covenant to repair the demised premises, it is necessarily a question of construction whether a boundary wall forms part of the demised premises. If it does not, the covenant does not apply to it (*Blundell v Newlands Investment Trust* (1958) 172 EG 855).

If the lease is silent, certain obligations will be implied in the case of a tenancy for a term of years (see below), and these may not accord with the parties' wishes. If the tenancy is from year to year or at will, no obligations will attach to either party, which makes the position clear but not satisfactory. The covenants in a 'new tenancy'—which is one granted after on or after 1 January 1996, unless it was granted pursuant to an agreement made or an option granted before that date—bind and benefit the landlord and tenant for the time being. Predecessors in title generally cease to be bound by the covenants and cannot enforce them (Landlord and Tenant (Covenants) Act 1995).

In relation to earlier leases, the LPA 1925, ss 141 and 142, provides that the benefits of tenants' covenants and the burden of landlord's covenants, where they have reference to the subject-matter of the lease, run with the reversion, so benefiting and binding whomsoever is in the position of landlord. Covenants which 'touch and concern' the land demised run with the land at common law, binding the tenant for the time being, and the benefit of the landlord's covenants runs similarly. Fencing covenants fall within both these definitions, and so remain valid and enforceable against and by the persons then concerned with the land, although one or both of the original parties to the lease have disposed of their interests. There is one possible exception. It may be that a covenant to erect a new fence or boundary wall (rather than merely to repair), in a lease executed prior to 1926, will not bind the tenant's successors in title unless he expressly covenanted for himself and his assigns (*Spence's Case* (1583) 5 Co Rep 16a). No difficulty arises in the case of covenants to repair only.

There is no limit to the period for which a fencing covenant in a lease can be effective (the rule against perpetuities not being applicable), so the covenant settles the question of fencing for the duration of the term. Although, formerly, a fencing covenant in a lease could only be enforced by the other party to the lease, a landlord's responsibility for a fence in a dangerous condition is in effect extended by the Defective Premises Act 1972, s 4. Anyone who might reasonably be expected to be affected by defects and who suffers injury or damage, has a remedy against a landlord who knew, or ought to have known, of the defect. A landlord who has reserved a right of entry to repair is, for this purpose only, treated as having covenanted to repair.

(b) *Agricultural Holdings*

Special provisions apply to the letting of an agricultural holding (Agricultural Holdings Act 1986), but not to a farm business tenancy (Agricultural Tenancies Act 1995). Most lettings of agricultural property on or after 1 September 1995 are therefore not affected.

Where these provisions do apply and the terms on which an agricultural holding is let do not expressly deal with fences and walls, certain covenants are implied (Agriculture (Maintenance,

Repair and Insurance of Fixed Equipment) Regulations 1973, Sched). The landlord must execute all repairs and replacements of walls and fences of open and covered yards and garden walls (para 1). The tenant has a duty to repair and leave in good repair, order and condition, various parts of the property, but only to the extent that the matters are not already covered by a landlord's covenant. The tenant's responsibility extends to fences, hedges, field walls, stiles, gates and posts (para 5 (1)). Also, he must cut, trim or lay a proper proportion of the hedges each year so as to maintain them in good and sound condition (para 9). These implied covenants are displaced by any written agreement placing responsibility on the other party (*Burden v Hannaford* [1956] 1 QB 143). In determining the extent of the implied obligation, regard must be had to the age, character and condition of the property at the beginning of the tenancy (*Evans v Jones* [1955] 2 QB 58).

In default, the other party may do the work and recover the reasonable cost from the other, although the amount the tenant can recover is limited to the smaller of £2,000 and the annual rent (paras 4(2), 12(2)). Breach of a covenant to maintain fences can also be the foundation of a notice to quit under the Agricultural Holdings Act 1986, Sched 3, Pt I, Case D (*Shepherd v Lomas* [1963] 1 WLR 962).

(c) Short residential lettings

The Landlord and Tenant Act 1985, s 11, implies repairing covenants on the part of the landlord into almost all short tenancies of residential property. However, it is unlikely that a garden wall or fence would be affected (*Hopwood v Cannock Chase District Council* [1975] 1 WLR 373).

(d) Covenants implied at common law

Apart from express provisions in the lease and the statutory provisions relating to agricultural holdings, the occupier of premises let for a term of years is liable to repair fences, but tenants from year to year or at will are not. This is because only tenants for years are liable for permissive waste. The landlord can maintain an action against the tenant where the repairs are not carried out, on the ground of damage to his inheritance (*Cheetham v Hampson* (1791) 4 Term Rep 318), and if the fences fall down by reason of excavations in breach of covenant a mandatory injunction may be granted to renew them (*Newton v Nock* (1880) 43 LT 197). Provided the landlord has not undertaken to repair the fences and (unless the tenant has agreed to put them in good repair) they were not dilapidated at the start of the term, the occupier is liable to any third party injured because of the want of repair.

For the performance of his obligations the occupier is entitled to fell timber (ie oak, ash and elm over 20 years old, and possibly other wood by local custom), the felling of which is generally waste. The use is known as 'estovers', but only felling for immediate fencing requirements is permitted.

(e) Compensation

Compensation is payable to the outgoing tenant of an agricultural holding in respect of improvements taking the form of the making or removal of permanent fences (Agricultural Holdings Act 1986, Scheds 7, 8). If the improvement was begun before 1 March 1948 (an 'old improvement'), the landlord's consent must have been obtained. For later improvements (a 'new improvement'), the tenant must either have the landlord's consent or the Minister's approval. A tenant who is aggrieved by his landlord withholding consent may apply to the Agricultural Land Tribunal (s 67(3)). The amount of compensation for an old improvement is such sum as fairly represents its value to an incoming tenant (Sched 9, Pt I, para 2(1)). For a new improvement, compensation equals the increase in the value of the holding attributable to the improvement, having regard to the character and situation of the holding and the average requirements of tenants reasonably skilled in husbandry (s 66(1)).

The tenant under a farm business tenancy is also entitled to compensation when he quits for improvements which he made at his own expense with his landlord's consent (Agricultural Tenancies Act 1995, s 17). The amount of it equals the increase in the value of the property at the end of the tenancy attributable to the improvement (s 20).

4 Fencing easements

A landowner may acquire an easement for his neighbour to fence the boundary between their properties, or to maintain a hedge along it (*Jones v Price* [1965] 2 QB 618). The duty arises when the work is not done for the benefit of the person doing it, but rather for his neighbour's benefit (*Hudson v Tabor* (1877) 2 QBD 290, 292 per Lord Coleridge CJ).

This is not an easement which is covered by the Prescription Act 1832, so title to the right must be made in other ways. This could be eg under the LPA 1925, s 62 on a conveyance by the former owner of the dominant and servient tenements (*Crow v Wood* [1971] 1 QB 77), or by prescription at common law. The latter theoretically involves proof that the right dates back to the limit of legal memory, 1189. In practice a long period of exercise of the right is accepted if there is no definite proof that the right previously did not exist. Alternatively, the court may apply the doctrine of the lost modern grant: ie the presumption that the duty must have been imposed by a document now lost. In either case proof of 20 or 30 years' undisputed exercise of the right is likely to succeed in the absence of evidence to the contrary. A right is normally established by proof that the owner of the servient tenement and his predecessors in title have been in the habit of carrying out all necessary repairs to the fence at their own expense, and doing so on receiving notice to do so from the owner of the dominant tenement and his predecessors.

It is interesting to contrast two cases. Evidence that the owners of one piece of land had repaired a certain fence for 50 years was held insufficient to establish an easement, in the absence of any evidence that they did so as a result of an obligation (*Hilton v Ankesson* (1872) 27 LT 519). On the other hand, evidence that a fence had been repaired by one party and his predecessors for 40 years was held sufficient, when combined with the fact that for the last 19 years they had done so on notice from those claiming the benefit of the easement (*Lawrence v Jenkins* (1873) LR 8 QB 274).

The landowner subject to the obligation is not entitled to notice of the want of repair. He is liable for all resulting damage, including escape of his neighbour's cattle, even though he was ignorant of the need for repair. He is not liable for the results of damage to the fence by act of God or *vis major*. Where the servient tenement is let, the action in cases of non-repair is against the tenant, not the landlord (*Lawrence v Jenkins* (1873) LR 8 QB 274).

No obligation can arise by prescription whereby one owner has to maintain a wall merely to protect his neighbour's building against penetration of the weather. This is not a right susceptible of constituting an easement (*Phipps v Pears* [1965] 1 QB 76). If, however, a wall is laid bare in the course of demolition, the local authority may require that the demolisher make it weatherproof (Public Health Act 1961, s 29). The neighbouring owner may also be able to exercise rights under the Party Wall etc Act 1996.

A prescriptive obligation to fence comes to an end if the dominant and servient tenements come into the same ownership, in such a way that the estate for which each is held is identical (*Canham v Fisk* (1831) 2 C & J 126).

5 Obligations arising from particular circumstances

(a) Land adjoining a highway

At common law there was no duty to fence a boundary with a highway*. This formerly meant that there was no liability for damage caused by animals straying on to the road. Now, however, the normal rules apply (Animals Act 1971, s 8). There are exceptions. Merely placing animals on unfenced land does not, without more, constitute a breach of duty if the person had the right to place animals on the land and that land is common land, is situated in an area where fencing is not customary, or is a town or village green. The keeper of any horses, cattle, sheep, goats or swine—the person in whose possession they are—commits an offence if they stray onto the highway, except where it passes over common, waste or unenclosed ground. Maximum fines are: £200 (first offence), £500 (thereafter) (Highways Act 1980, s 155).

The Highways Act 1980, s 165, imposes an obligation upon the owner of land adjoining a street (which includes *inter alia* a highway, lane, footpath or passage, whether a thoroughfare or not) adequately to fence anything thereon which is a source of danger to persons using the street (as, for example, a building in the course of demolition). This is enforced by the local authority serving on the owner notice to execute the necessary works and, subject to an appeal to the magistrates' court, on his failure to comply the authority may carry out the work at the owner's expense. Where the only source of danger is the difference in level between the road and the adjoining land, the owner cannot be compelled to fence because the danger does not exist in or on his land (*Myers v Harrow Corporation* [1962] 2 QB 442). There are also statutory obligations

---

* In fact, from the reign of Edward I to that of George III it was forbidden to maintain a dyke, tree or bush 'whereby a man may work to do hurt' within 200 feet of either side of a highway, as a protection against highwaymen, rogues and vagabonds (*Searle v Wallbank* [1947] AC 341, 347–8).

to fence certain objects of danger within certain distances of a road, such as steam engines, windmills and dangerous quarries.

Where a fence has been erected adjoining a highway, liability will arise if it is allowed to fall into such a state of dilapidation that it is a nuisance, and any person using the highway is injured as a natural result (*Harrold v Watney* [1898] 2 QB 320). This can also be a nuisance which magistrates, on the complaint of a local authority, can order to be abated (Public Health Act 1961, ss 24, 25).

Where the land adjoining a highway is fenced with barbed wire, or the fence contains barbed wire, which is a nuisance to the highway (ie if it is likely to be injurious to persons or animals lawfully using the highway), the highway authority can serve a notice on the occupier to abate the nuisance within a specified time (not less than one month nor more than six months) (Highways Act 1980, s 164). If the highway authority is itself the occupier any ratepayer can initiate similar action.

A fence which is dangerous to persons lawfully using the highway can also lead to a civil action for nuisance. Actions have been brought successfully where the injury was caused by wire (*Stewart v Wright* (1893) 9 TLR 480) and by spikes (*Morrison v Sheffield Corporation* [1917] 2 KB 866).

Where a hedge, tree or shrub overhangs any road or footpath to which the public has access and endangers, obstructs or interferes with the passage or view of vehicle drivers or pedestrians or the light from a public lamp, the appropriate authority may require it to be lopped within 14 days or (subject to an appeal to the magistrates' court) do it themselves at the owner's or occupier's expense (Highways Act 1980, s 154).

No door, gate or bar on any premises may open outwards on a street, except in the case of a public building with the consent of the local authority and the highway authority. An owner may be given eight days in which to alter an offending door, and in default is subject to a fine of £200 (Highways Act 1980, s 153).

It is an offence (carrying a fine of up to £500) to erect a fence or plant a hedge in a highway which consists of or comprises a carriageway for vehicles (Highways Act 1980, s 138). A person interested in land adjoining or near a highway may enter into an agreement with the highway authority restricting or regulating the use of the land, and in particular what grows on it. The agreement is registrable as a local land charge (Highways Act 1980, s 253).

Vaults, arches and cellars under streets must be kept in good repair. In default, the local authority may do necessary work and recover the expense (Highways Act 1980, s 180(6), (7)). A person injured has no action against a defaulter (*Scott v Green & Sons* [1969] 1 WLR 301).

A highway authority, may, and in some circumstances must, fence the highway. If a fence protecting highway users from a dangerous drop, or a stream, is part of the highway—which is a question of fact as to whether it is built on land originally dedicated or acquired for the highway—it is repairable with the highway (*R v Whitney* (1835) 7 C & P 208). Where the authority, or its predecessors in title, have fenced a dangerous place, it may be liable for damage resulting from removal of the fence (*Whyler v Bingham Rural Council* [1901] 1 KB 45). A highway authority may erect and maintain a fence to prevent access to a road. This power may not, however, be exercised in such a way as to interfere with a gate used for agricultural purposes, a public right of way, or a means of access to the road for which planning permission has been granted or for which it was not needed because it existed on 1 July 1948 and did not contravene the earlier legislation (Highways Act 1980, s 80). In any area of the countryside where walls of a particular construction are a feature, the highway authority's powers and duties relating to fences can apply to walls of that construction (Wildlife and Countryside Act 1981, s 72(12)). A special road authority may stop up private means of access to special roads (eg motorways) and provide alternative means of access to adjoining premises (1980 Act, s 125).

(b) Land accessible to the public

A local authority has power to require works, which may include fencing, to remove the danger from an excavation on land accessible to the public from a highway, or on a place of public resort. In default, or where the authority does not know the identity of the owner or occupier of the land, it must carry out the work required (Local Government (Miscellaneous Provisions) Act 1976, s 25).

(c) Land adjoining a common

An owner of land adjoining a common may, by prescription, become liable to fence his property against the beasts grazing on the common, although only with a fence capable of keeping out the type which usually graze there (*Coaker v Willocks* [1911] 2 KB 124). Breach of such an obligation gives rise to at least a claim for nominal damages by the owner of cattle which stray off the common (*Egerton v Harding* [1975] QB 62).

(d) Animals

The owner of livestock (cattle, horses, asses, mules, hinnies, sheep, pigs, goats, poultry, deer not in the wild state, and captive pheasants, partridges and grouse) is liable for any damage to land or property that it causes when it strays on to someone else's land (Animals Act 1971, s 4). The owner is also liable for the cost of maintaining the livestock before it is restored to him. For this purpose, the person who has possession of the livestock is liable as owner. There is no liability where the animals stray from the highway, provided their presence there was a lawful use of the highway (s 5(5)).

The fact that the land on to which the animals strayed was not fenced is not of itself a defence. But the livestock owner is not liable if he can establish that the animals would not have strayed but for a breach of a duty to fence by someone interested in the land (s 5(6)). The duty to fence does not have to be owed to the livestock owner. It could be an obligation attached to the freehold or a covenant in a lease.

A landowner has a duty of care to users of an adjoining highway to prevent stock known to be on the land from straying. But when a heifer strayed from land let on a grass keep agreement and caused an accident, the landowner was not liable because there was no evidence that he knew the fencing to be inadequate (*Hoskin v Rogers* (1985) *The Times*, 25 January).

If any horses, cattle, sheep, goats or swine are found straying or lying on or at the side of the highway, their keeper (the person in whose possession they are) is liable to a fine of up to £200 (first offence) or £500 (thereafter) (Highways Act 1980, s 155). This does not apply where the highway crosses common, waste or unenclosed land, and is without prejudice to any right of pasture on the side of the highway. However, there was an offence where a cow strayed from common land onto a road and went 300 yards along the road away from the common, where a car collided with it (*Rees v Morgan* (1960) *The Times*, 14 February).

(e) Dangerous objects and operations

The occupier of land used for dangerous operations or for the storage of dangerous objects must consider fencing obligations from two points of view: to prevent the escape from his land of dangerous things, or objects made dangerous by the activities on his land, and to prevent the entry of persons who are likely to be harmed there.

The rule in *Rylands v Fletcher* (1868) LR 3 HL 330, imposes upon the occupier of land a strict liability for the results of the escape from that land of dangerous objects not normally there, or accumulated there in unnatural quantities. No negligence is necessary. Act of God, statutory authority, act of a third party and consent or default of the injured party are defences.

Apart from this an occupier may be liable under the general law of negligence for the results of the escape of something from his land, such as a golf ball (*Castle v St Augustine's Links* (1922) 38 TLR 615), or a football (*Hilder v Associated Portland Cement Manufacturers Ltd* [1961] 1 WLR 1434). This is not an absolute liability; it depends upon whether he could reasonably have foreseen what happened, which is a question of fact. The number of times similar things have happened before and the cost of preventing it are relevant (*Bolton v Stone* [1951] AC 850).

The Occupiers' Liability Act 1957, s 2, imposes upon the occupier of premises the duty to take such care as in all the circumstances of the case is reasonable to see that a visitor will be reasonably safe using the premises for the purpose for which he has been invited or permitted to be there. As permission to enter will be assumed in cases where people habitually use the premises, although not expressly authorised, the obligation will probably only be discharged by the erection and maintenance of fences to exclude them where the premises are themselves inherently dangerous (such as a deep gravel pit). The Act expressly states as an example that, in assessing whether a degree of care is reasonable in any case, consideration should be given to the fact that children are less careful than adults, and accordingly it may be more necessary to fence against them. Where premises are occupied for business purposes, the occupier cannot exclude his liability for breach of this common duty of care in so far as it results in death or personal injury, and can only do so in the case of other loss if in all the circumstances it is reasonable (Unfair Contract Terms Act 1977, ss 1, 2).

6 Statutory obligations

(a) Railways

The Railways Clauses Consolidation Act 1845, s 68, imposed upon railway companies acquiring land compulsorily the obligation to fence it in perpetuity as part of the accommodation works. This duty persists and now falls on Railtrack plc (Railways Act 1993). It even continues after the land has ceased to be used for railway purposes (*R Walker & Son v British Railways Board* [1984] 1 WLR 805).

The extent of the duty to fence is limited. The obligation is to mark the limit of railway property. There is no general duty to fence in such a way as to exclude adult or child trespassers (*Proffitt v British Railways Board* (1985) *The Times*, 4 February).

The original acquiring companies were, however, empowered to pay compensation in return for a release from their fencing obligations where the vendor agreed. Many such releases were in fact effected. It is not always clear today, however, whether or not this happened in respect of any particular stretch of line, because the railways do still maintain some fences where they are not obliged to. Normally where a release was granted it was stated in the conveyance of the land to the railway company, but even if a duplicate or counterpart conveyance was executed then, it may be that because of the lapse of time, no record of the release now appears on the title. It is therefore wise to make enquiries about this when buying or taking a lease of land bordering a railway.

Anyone using an accommodation way across a railway must close and fasten any gate, or lower any barrier, as soon as he has driven over or taken animals across. Failure to do so is an offence (fine up to £1,000) (Railway Clauses Consolidation Act 1845, s 75; Transport and Works Act 1992, s 49).

(b) Parsonages

Church of England incumbents are required, by order of the Parsonages Board or the Diocesan Board of Finance, to carry out repairs, specified by the diocesan surveyor, to the walls, fences and gates of the parsonage house and any former parsonage house while vested in them (Repair of Benefice Buildings Measure 1972, ss 2–6; Endowments and Glebe Measure 1976, s 33).

(c) Churchyards and burial grounds

The parochial church council or the burial board, as the case may be, must maintain the boundary walls and fences of a disused churchyard or burial ground. Upon their certifying the cost of the repairs, they are entitled to repayment from the general rates, except where there is another fund legally chargeable with the expense (Burial Act 1855, s 18; Parochial Church Councils (Powers) Measure 1921; Rating and Valuation Act 1925, s 4). A cemetery company is bound to maintain the boundary walls and fences of a cemetery in good repair and, in the absence of special provisions, these must be substantial walls or iron railings at least eight feet high (Cemeteries Clauses Act 1847).

(d) Disused mines

The owner of an abandoned mine, or one that has not been worked for 12 months, must fence it, to prevent injury to persons or animals falling down the shaft (Mines and Quarries Act 1954, s 151).

(e) Local legislation

In some areas, local authorities have powers under local Acts to oblige owners to repair boundary walls and fences. In Manchester, eg, a district council can require the repair, replacement or renewal of a party or boundary wall or fence of any house, if it has collapsed, is in danger of collapsing, or is in a ruinous or dilapidated condition (Greater Manchester Act 1981, s 43(1)).

7 Obligation not to fence

Some conveyances and leases contain covenants not to fence specified boundaries. This is common enough on modern housing estates laid out with open plan front gardens. A mandatory injunction is the appropriate remedy for the removal of a fence erected in contravention of such a covenant, but it will not be issued in every case (*Shepherd Homes Ltd v Sandham* [1971] Ch 340). However, there is no need to show that the plaintiff has suffered loss, or that the defendant has made a profit, before a mandatory injunction will be issued (*Harlow Development Corporation v Myers* [1979] 1 EGLR 143 (CC).

Chapter 6

Rights of Entry

1 Common law position

There is no general right to enter neighbouring property to repair a boundary fence or a flank wall, even if that is the most convenient, or even the only practicable, means of doing it (*Kwiatkowski v Cox* [1970] EGD 9). An owner who enters to repair without authority can be restrained by injunction (*John Trenbarth Ltd v National Westminster Bank Ltd* (1969) 39 P & CR 104).

There are, however, a number of ways in which a landowner may be authorised to enter to do repairs.

(a) Express agreement

The owner of the land which the fence owner needs to enter can of course give permission. That consent may be for a single occasion, for a limited period or permanent. If it is to bind the successors in title of the person granting permission it will need to constitute an easement. Should the grant not take effect as a legal easement—because it is not granted in fee simple or for a term of years absolute or it is not granted by deed—and yet it is still a right of the same nature, it should be protected by registration. It can be registered as an equitable easement, land charge class D(iii), or protected on the land register by a notice or caution.

A landlord who covenants in a lease to repair fences on the demised premises has an implied right of entry to do the work (*Saner v Bilton* (1878) 7 Ch D 815). This may also apply even if the landlord has not undertaken an obligation to repair, but both parties expect him to do the work (*Mint v Good* [1951] 1 KB 517).

If it was the tenant who covenanted to repair, and he does not, the landlord can only enter the property to make good the default if he expressly reserved the right to do so (*Regional Properties Ltd v City of London Real Property Co Ltd; Sedgwick Forbes Bland Payne Group Ltd v Regional Properties Ltd* [1981] 1 EGLR 33).

(b) Implied authority

A right of access can arise by prescription, even if that has the effect of placing a restriction on the use to which the neighbour can put the strip of land (*Ward v Kirkland* [1967] Ch 194).

In the same case it was suggested, although somewhat tentatively, that the doctrine that a person may not derogate from his grant, would also apply. So, where part of a property is sold off, including a wall on the boundary common to the seller and buyer, the buyer may enter the retained land to maintain his property. It may not be necessary to rely on that doctrine, because the LPA 1925, s 62, implying the general words into a conveyance, will have the effect of vesting a right of entry in the buyer.

(c) Party walls

As has already been mentioned, one joint owner of a party wall has the right to enter his neighbour's property to carry out repairs (p 51) and there are statutory rights under the Party Wall etc Act 1996.

2 Statutory rights

(a) Access to neighbouring land

The provisions of the Access to Neighbouring Land Act 1992 are dealt with separately below.

(b) Landlord and tenant: residential property

A number of statutes regulating particular types of residential tenancy give the landlord a right of entry to do the repairs he is entitled to do. It is to be noted that that authority goes beyond merely the repairs which a statute obliges the landlord to do, and indeed beyond the work he covenants to do. This condition applies to assured tenancies (Housing Act 1988, s 16), protected tenancies (Rent Act 1977, s 148) and statutory tenancies of agricultural tied accommodation (Rent (Agriculture) Act 1976, Sched 5, para 8).

(c) Party Wall etc Act 1996

The rights of entry conferred by this Act have been dealt with earlier (pp 50–52).

3 Access to Neighbouring Land Act 1992

(a) General scheme

The object of the 1992 Act is to provide a way in which a landowner who lacks authority to enter neighbouring land to do necessary work to his own property can obtain that authority. In the absence of agreement, he may apply to court for an access order which will permit him to enter. An agreement purporting to exclude or restrict someone's right to apply for an access order is void (s 4(4)).

The Act does not extend to authorising entry onto a highway for the purpose of doing works (s 8(3): definition of 'land'), nor to entry onto Crown land, as the Act is not stated to bind the Crown.

The right to apply for an order is deliberately confined to those who do not have the neighbour's consent (s 1(1)). In a case where consent has already been given, but the landowner does not wish to avail himself of it—perhaps because he is required to make a payment, or because it requires work to be done in a particular way which is not the most convenient—there is no additional statutory right.

The landowner must also justify the need for an order. The work must be 'reasonably necessary for the preservation' of all or part of his property, and it has to be impossible or substantially more difficult to carry out without going on the neighbouring land (s 1(2)). In addition, there is an overall prohibition on making an order if it would be unreasonable, having regard to the degree of interference or disturbance with the use or enjoyment of the neighbouring land, or the hardship suffered by the occupier (s 1(3)).

The way in which the order achieves its purpose is to require the respondent, so far as he has the power, to permit the applicant and those whom he may reasonably authorise ('his associates') to enter and do the work which it authorises. They can, unless the order modifies these rights, take reasonably necessary materials, plant and equipment onto the neighbouring land, leave them there for the period during which the work is permitted, removing them at the end of that time (s 3(1), (2), (7)).

Merely preventing the respondent to the applicant's action from taking action for trespass or nuisance against the applicant begs the question who is entitled to object to the work being done. There may, of course, be more than one person with rights in the neighbouring property which allow him to do so, eg the freeholder, the leaseholder and the person entitled to a right of way. It is the applicant who must decide with whose consent he needs to dispense by obtaining an order. Careful enquiries should be made before applying for an order to ensure that all who legitimately oppose the entry are made respondents. If it is not reasonably possible to ascertain the identity of the person who should be made respondent, the applicant may be able to apply for an order against that person by description rather than name. There is power to make rules of court to that effect (s 4(3)), but no rules have yet been made.

(b) Work to be done

The statutory scheme is confined to work reasonably necessary to preserve all or part of the property in question (s 1(2)).

This is amplified by a provision which automatically covers what the Act calls 'basic preservation works' which it is reasonably necessary to carry out. These basic preservation works include a number of items relevant here: first, the maintenance, repair or renewal of any part of a building or other structure, which would cover boundary walls and fences; secondly, the treatment, cutting back, felling, removal or replacement of any hedge, tree or shrub, when damaged, diseased, dangerous, insecurely rooted or dead, or becoming so; and thirdly, filling in or clearing a ditch (s 1(4)).

Work is not necessarily ruled out because it involves either making an alteration, adjustment or improvement or demolition. The court must, in such a case, consider it fair and reasonable in all the circumstances (s 1(5)). Consequential work can be authorised, and that includes inspection to ascertain whether work is needed, doing surveys and plotting the position of services (s 1(6), (7)).

(c) Application for an order

An application for an access order is made to a county court (procedure: CCR O 49, r 1), although the High Court and the county court have concurrent jurisdiction (s 7).

For an access order to be made, the court must be satisfied on

three points (subs (1)–(3)):
(1) The applicant does not already have the necessary consent to enter the adjoining land for that purpose.
(2) The work cannot be carried out without entering the other land, or that would make it substantially more difficult.
(3) The entry on the land will not, to a degree that would make it unreasonable to make the order, interfere with or disturb anyone's use or enjoyment of the adjoining land or cause anyone who occupies all or part of it to suffer hardship. These considerations are not merely confined to the respondent to the court application. This consideration overrides condition (2).

(d) Terms of order

There are three matters which an access order has to specify (s 2(1)). It must state what works the applicant may carry out from the neighbouring property, onto what part of the property he is authorised to enter and when and for how long entry is allowed. The order also places three positive duties on the applicant (s 3(3)). First, he must ensure that waste is removed from the neighbouring land forthwith. Secondly, he must, so far as reasonably practicable, make that land good before the period during which entry is authorised expires. Finally, he has to indemnify the respondent against damage to the land or to goods which would not have been caused had the order not been made.

Conditions can be placed on the order, to avoid or restrict loss, damage, injury, inconvenience or loss of privacy. In particular, there can be conditions about the way the work is to be done, the days and time of the work, who may enter, and the precautions to be taken (s 2(2), (3)). The order may restrict applicant's rights to take materials, plant and equipment on the neighbouring land (s 3(4)).

The court can also require the applicant to reimburse expenses which the respondent incurs in connection with the application and which cannot otherwise be recovered as costs. It can also order the applicant to give security for payment of compensation (see below) or of sums under the indemnity he gives for damage caused (s 2(9)).

(e) Compensation

Where an access order is made to permit work on non-residential land, the applicant can be required to pay the respondent compensation (s 2(5)–(8)). It is the nature of the applicant's property which governs whether compensation is payable, not the nature of the land on which he goes to do the work. For this purpose, residential land is property which is a dwelling, or part of one, and other parts of a building used mainly with any dwelling in it. It extends to a garden, yard, private garage or outbuilding used or enjoyed wholly or mainly with a dwelling.

The amount of compensation is what is fair and reasonable having regard to two factors:

(1) The financial benefit to the applicant and connected person (the owner of any estate or interest in the property on which the work is to be done, or any right over it, any occupier of that property or anyone whom the applicant can reasonably permit to enter for the work authorised by the order). This is whichever is the greater of: either the amount by which the value of the applicant's land is likely to rise as a result of doing the work, less the cost of the work; or the difference in the cost of work if done without entering the neighbouring property and the cost with the benefit of the access order.

(2) The degree of inconvenience which the entry is likely to cause to the respondent or others.

(f) Successors in title

The benefit of an access order belongs only to the applicant; it does not extend to the owners of other interests in the property, nor to the applicant's successors in title.

On the other hand, an order may be binding on the respondent's successors, ie later owners of the neighbouring land. To the extent that the court considers it just and equitable, they have power to enforce the order and its terms and conditions, so eg a later owner may claim compensation (s 4(2)).

In principle, an order binds the respondent's successors and anyone deriving title under him whose estate or interest was created after the order was made (s 4(1)). The class of people whom the order affects would therefore include those who buy and inherit the land from the respondent and tenants under leases which he created after the date of the order. However, the extent to which successors in title are bound is affected by the rules relating to registration.

An application for an access order comes into the category of pending land action and an order when made is registrable in the register of writs and orders affecting land (Land Charges Act 1972, ss 5(1)(*a*), 6(1)(*a*); 1992 Act, s 5(1), (6)). In the case of registered land, an application and an order may be protected by the registration of a notice or a caution; the fact that the applicant is in actual occupation of any of the neighbouring land does not make the rights under an order an overriding interest (Land Registration Act 1925, ss 49(1)(*j*), 59(1), (2), 70(1)(*g*); 1992 Act, s 5(2), (5)).

If an application for an order is not registered and the neighbouring land is sold, the effect on the buyer varies depending upon whether the title is registered. If it is, the buyer is not bound by it even though he has notice of it (Land Registration Act 1925, s 59(6)). In the case of unregistered land, a buyer only takes free from an unregistered application if he does not know of it (Land Charges Act 1972, s 5(7)). Once an order has been made, it must be registered if it is to bind a buyer (1925 Act, s 59(6); 1972 Act, s 6(4)).

(*g*) *Agreements instead of orders*

Neighbours will normally wish to negotiate access to do work from adjoining property rather than having to obtain a court order, even if the negotiations are conducted in the shadow of the Act. However, it is open to question whether the parties can effectively obtain the same benefits for themselves without resort to the court.

A property owner can, of course, at any time agree that his neighbour may enter his land for a specified purpose either free or on terms. But that is an arrangement between those particular parties. An access order confers two important further benefits: first, provided it is registered, it will bind future owners of the neighbouring land; and secondly, those future owners will be able to enforce the positive obligations which bind the applicant, eg reinstatement and the payment of compensation. It should be possible in drafting the agreement to allow the neighbour's successors in title to enforce it, but it will not always be possible to guarantee that those successors are bound by the agreement.

If the rights created by an agreement are to be made binding on the neighbouring owner's successor, they will have to create an interest known to the law and be capable of protection on the register. They may constitute an equitable easement or the agreement may be an estate contract ('a contract ... to convey or create a legal estate': Land Charges Act 1972, s 2(4)(iv)), in which case there is no problem. But the terms of the agreement may not allow it to fall within either of these categories, in which case successors may well not be bound.

Those who are seeking rights of entry to repair, and their advisers, may therefore consider that, except in minor cases where there will be no delay, applying for a formal access order offers definite advantages.

(h) Impact of the Act on other provisions

In one application to a leasehold valuation tribunal to approve the terms of a management scheme for a central London estate, for the purposes of leasehold enfranchisement (Leasehold Reform, Housing and Urban Development Act 1993, s 70), the proposed scheme included rights of entry when necessary to repair neighbouring property. Objectors argued that the 1992 Act rendered that unnecessary. However, the scheme was improved with that provision included (*Re Grosvenor Estate (Mayfair) London's Application* [1995] 2 EGLR 201 (LVT)). Presumably, this recognised that the statutory rights—involving an application to court each time they are to be exercised, and being subject to a discretion as to the reasonableness of making an order—are less satisfactory for the 'dominant' landowner than an absolute entitlement to enter.

Chapter 7

Miscellaneous

1 Planning

The erection of walls and fences is an operation that is within the definition of development in the Town and Country Planning Act 1990, s 55, and accordingly permission is necessary before it can lawfully be done. General permission is, however, given for the erection of certain fences, etc, by the Town and Country Planning (General Permitted Development) Order 1995. This deems permission to have been given for the erection of gates, fences, walls and other means of inclosure that do not exceed one metre in height when adjacent to a road used by vehicles, or two metres in height in other cases. There seems to be no authority as to how far back from the road a side wall has to be before it can be said not to be adjacent to the road. An inspector hearing an appeal against an enforcement notice decided that a fence 38cm back from a highway abutted it (the earlier expression) (T/APP/5337/C/82/1995/G4). To be covered by this provision, the wall must serve to enclose property. But if, in addition, it has another purpose (eg retaining banked soil) that does not prevent the consent from applying (*Prengate Properties Ltd v Secretary of State for the Environment* (1973) 25 P & CR 311).

The permission granted by the Order may be removed in certain cases by a direction of the local planning authority confirmed by the Secretary of State. One of the agreed standard enquiries to accompany local land charges searches to all local authorities asks whether such a direction applies to the property in question. A condition imposed on a planning consent can also have the effect of negating the general permission.

A fence may in some circumstances be erected as a wind-break for agricultural purposes. It is then permitted agricultural development (*Cotswold District Council v Secretary of State for the Environment* (1993) EGCS 49).

Erecting a parapet wall around a flat roof over a house extension constitutes the enlargement of the house requiring permission, unless it is within the limits permitted by the Order (*Richmond London Borough Council v Secretary of State for the Environment* [1991] EGCS 37).

The formation or laying out of means of access to highway is also an operation that requires planning permission. This applies to access, whether private or public, for vehicles or pedestrians. It extends to all streets, but the Order gives an automatic consent where the road is not a classified one and the work is required in connection with development for which permission has been given.

2 Settled land

(a) Duty to fence

In the absence of a direction in the trust instrument, a tenant for life is not bound, by virtue of his position as such, to erect or repair fences on the boundaries of the settled property (*Re Cartwright* (1889) 41 Ch D 532; *Woodhouse v Walker* (1880) 5 QBD 404), except where the settled land is leasehold and the lease casts the obligation on the tenant. As occupier of the property, however, he has the normal obligations under the general law, outlined in Chapter 5. On the other hand, unless the trust instrument expressly gives him an interest 'without impeachment of waste' the tenant for life is liable for 'voluntary waste', which would include the positive action of destroying a boundary fence. Damages are recoverable for the injury done by an act of waste, and any person interested under the settlement may apply for an injunction to prevent it, and may sue under RSC Ord 15, r 13, on behalf of himself and all persons having the same interest.

(b) Erection of fences

The erection of a fence is one of the improvements that a tenant for life for the purposes of the Settled Land Act 1925 may carry out and have paid for from capital money without being called upon to repay by instalments. The scheme for improvements does not have to be submitted by the tenant for life for prior approval by the trustees or the court. The trustees are authorised to pay out the money on the certificate of the tenant for life's engineer or surveyor. The settled land may be mortgaged to raise money for this purpose.

3 Trusts of Land

Trustees of land normally have all the powers of an absolute owner of property (Trusts of Land and Appointment of Trustees Act 1996, s 6(1)). This is subject to two qualifications. First, the powers must not be exercised in contravention of any other Act, rule of law or equity, or order including an order of the Charity Commissioners (s 6(6)–(8)). Secondly, a disposition creating a trust, such as a conveyance to more than one person, may validly restrict the trustees' powers (s 8).

4 Churchyards

The special legal rules which govern the property of the Church of England affect the fixing and fencing of the boundaries of churchyards. The care and maintenance of a churchyard is the responsibility of the parochial church council (Parochial Church Council (Powers) Measure 1956, s 4(ii)(c)), and that includes taking proceedings to settle boundary disputes where necessary (*St Edmundsbury and Ipswich Diocesan Board of Finance v Clark (No 2)* [1973] 1 WLR 1572).

A faculty, granted by the chancellor of the diocese, is required for works in a churchyard, and this includes the erection of a boundary fence or wall. This applies both to consecrated and unconsecrated churchyards (Faculty Jurisdiction Measure 1964, s 7). A faculty will not be granted until it is established precisely where the boundary runs, so that the fence is erected in the right place (*Re St Peter and St Paul, Scrayingham* [1992] 1 WLR 187). However, in one case a faculty was granted to keep a fence where it was accepted that 'the present line of the fence represents a sensible demarcation line' (*Re St Clement's, Leigh-on-Sea* [1988] 1 WLR 720, 726). See also p 74.

Appendix 1

Statutes

Law of Property Act 1925

38 Party structures

(1) Where under a disposition or other arrangement which, if a holding in undivided shares had been permissible, would have created a tenancy in common, a wall or other structure is or is expressed to be made a party wall or structure, that structure shall be and remain severed vertically as between the respective owners, and the owner of each part shall have such rights to support and user over the rest of the structure as may be requisite for conferring rights corresponding to those which would have subsisted if a valid tenancy in common had been created.

(2) Any person interested may, in case of dispute, apply to the court for an order declaring the rights and interests under this section of the persons interested in any such party structure, and the court may make such order as it thinks fit.

* * * * *

Access to Neighbouring Land Act 1992

ARRANGEMENT OF SECTIONS

An Act to enable persons who desire to carry out works to any land which are reasonably necessary for the preservation of that land to obtain access to neighbouring land in order to do so; and for purposes connected therewith.   [16th March 1992]

1 Access orders

(1) A person—

(a) who, for the purpose of carrying out works to any land (the 'dominant land'), desires to enter upon any adjoining or adjacent land (the 'servient land'), and

(b) who needs, but does not have, the consent of some other person to that entry,

may make an application to the court for an order under this section ('an access order') against that other person.

(2) On an application under this section, the court shall make an access order if, and only if, it is satisfied—

(a) that the works are reasonably necessary for the preservation of the whole or any part of the dominant land; and

(b) that they cannot be carried out, or would be substantially more difficult to carry out, without entry upon the servient land;

but this subsection is subject to subsection (3) below.

(3) The court shall not make an access order in any case where it is satisfied that, were it to make such an order—

(a) the respondent or any other person would suffer interference with, or disturbance of, his use or enjoyment of the servient land, or

(b) the respondent, or any other person (whether of full age or capacity or not) in occupation of the whole or any part of the servient land, would suffer hardship,

to such a degree by reason of the entry (notwithstanding any requirement of this Act or any term or condition that may be imposed under it) that it would be unreasonable to make the order.

(4) Where the court is satisfied on an application under this section that it is reasonably necessary to carry out any basic preservation works to the dominant land, those works shall be taken for the purposes of this Act to be reasonably necessary for the preservation of the land; and in this subsection 'basic preservation works' means any of the following, that is to say—

(a) the maintenance, repair or renewal of any part of a building or other structure comprised in, or situate on, the dominant land;

(b) the clearance, repair or renewal of any drain, sewer, pipe or cable so comprised or situate;

(c) the treatment, cutting back, felling, removal or replacement of any hedge, tree, shrub or other growing thing which is so comprised and which is, or is in danger of becoming, damaged, diseased, dangerous, insecurely rooted or dead;

(d) the filling in, or clearance, of any ditch so comprised;

but this subsection is without prejudice to the generality of the works which may, apart from it, be regarded by the court as reasonably necessary for the preservation of any land.

(5) If the court considers it fair and reasonable in all the circumstances of the case, works may be regarded for the purposes of this Act as being reasonably necessary for the preservation of any land (or, for the purposes of subsection (4) above, as being basic preservation works which it is reasonably necessary to carry out to any land) notwithstanding that the works incidentally involve—

(a) the making of some alteration, adjustment or improvement to the land, or

(b) the demolition of the whole or any part of a building or structure comprised in or situate upon the land.

(6) Where any works are reasonably necessary for the preservation of the whole or any part of the dominant land, the doing to the dominant land of anything which is requisite for, incidental to, or consequential on, the carrying out of those works shall be treated for the purposes of this Act as the carrying out of works which are reasonably necessary for the preservation of that land; and references in this Act to works, or to the carrying out of works, shall be construed accordingly.

(7) Without prejudice to the generality of subsection (6) above, if it is reasonably necessary for a person to inspect the dominant land—

(a) for the purpose of ascertaining whether any works may be reasonably necessary for the preservation of the whole or any part of that land,

(b) for the purpose of making any map or plan, or ascertaining the course of any drain, sewer, pipe or cable, in preparation for, or otherwise in connection with, the carrying out of works which are so reasonably necessary, or

(c) otherwise in connection with the carrying out of any such works,

the making of such an inspection shall be taken for the purposes of this Act to be the carrying out to the dominant land of works which are reasonably necessary for the preservation of that land; and references in this Act to works, or to the carrying out of works, shall be construed accordingly.

2 Terms and conditions of access orders

(1) An access order shall specify—

(a) the works to the dominant land that may be carried out by entering upon the servient land in pursuance of the order;

(b) the particular area of servient land that may be entered upon by virtue of the order for the purpose of carrying out those works to the dominant land; and

(c) the date on which, or the period during which, the land may be so entered upon;

and in the following provisions of this Act any reference to the servient land is a reference to the area specified in the order in pursuance of paragraph (b) above.

(2) An access order may impose upon the applicant or the respondent such terms and conditions as appear to the court to be reasonably necessary for the purpose of avoiding or restricting—

(a) any loss, damage, or injury which might otherwise be caused to the respondent or any other person by reason of the entry authorised by the order; or

(b) any inconvenience or loss of privacy that might otherwise be so caused to the respondent or any other person.

(3) Without prejudice to the generality of subsection (2) above, the terms and conditions which may be imposed under that subsection include provisions with respect to—

(a) the manner in which the specified works are to be carried out;

(b) the days on which, and the hours between which, the work involved may be executed;

(c) the persons who may undertake the carrying out of the specified works or enter upon the servient land under or by virtue of the order;

(d) the taking of any such precautions by the applicant as may be specified in the order.

(4) An access order may also impose terms and conditions—

(a) requiring the applicant to pay, or to secure that such person connected with him as may be specified in the order pays, compensation for—

(i) any loss, damage or injury, or

(ii) any substantial loss of privacy or other substantial inconvenience,

which will, or might, be caused to the respondent or any other person by reason of the entry authorised by the order;

(b) requiring the applicant to secure that he, or such person connected with him as may be specified in the order, is insured against any such risks as may be so specified; or

(c) requiring such a record to be made of the condition of the servient land, or of such part of it as may be so specified, as the court may consider expedient with a view to facilitating the determination of any question that may arise concerning damage to that land.

(5) An access order may include provision requiring the applicant to pay the respondent such sum by way of consideration for the privilege of entering the servient land in pursuance of the order as appears to the court to be fair and reasonable having regard to all the circumstances of the case, including, in particular—

(a) the likely financial advantage of the order to the applicant and any persons connected with him; and

(b) the degree of inconvenience likely to be caused to the respondent or any other person by the entry;

but no payment shall be ordered under this subsection if and to the extent that the works which the applicant desires to carry out by means of the entry are works to residential land.

(6) For the purposes of subsection (5)(*a*) above, the likely financial advantage of an access order to the applicant and any persons connected with him shall in all cases be taken to be a sum of money equal to the greater of the following amounts, that is to say—

(*a*) the amount (if any) by which so much of any likely increase in the value of any land—

    (i)   which consists of or includes the dominant land, and

    (ii) which is owned or occupied by the same person as the dominant land,

as may reasonably be regarded as attributable to the carrying out of the specified works exceeds the likely cost of carrying out those works with the benefit of the access order; and

(*b*) the difference (if it would have been possible to carry out the specified works without entering upon the servient land) between—

    (i)   the likely cost of carrying out those works without entering upon the servient land; and

    (ii) the likely cost of carrying them out with the benefit of the access order.

(7) For the purposes of subsection (5) above, 'residential land' means so much of any land as consists of—

(*a*) a dwelling or part of a dwelling;

(*b*) a garden, yard, private garage or outbuilding which is used and enjoyed wholly or mainly with a dwelling; or

(*c*) in the case of a building which includes one or more dwellings, any part of the building which is used and enjoyed wholly or mainly with those dwellings or any of them.

(8) The persons who are to be regarded for the purposes of this section as 'connected with' the applicant are—

(*a*) the owner of any estate or interest in, or right over, the whole or any part of the dominant land;

(*b*) the occupier of the whole or any part of the dominant land; and

(*c*) any person whom the applicant may authorise under section 3(7) below to exercise the power of entry conferred by the access order.

(9) The court may make provision—

(*a*) for the reimbursement by the applicant of any expenses reasonably incurred by the respondent in connection with the application which are not otherwise recoverable as costs;

(*b*) for the giving of security by the applicant for any sum that might become payable to the respondent or any other person by virtue of this section or section 3 below.

3 Effect of access order

(1) An access order requires the respondent, so far as he has power to do so, to permit the applicant or any of his associates to do anything which the applicant or associate is authorised or required to do under or by virtue of the order or this section.

(2) Except as otherwise provided by or under this Act, an access order authorises the applicant or any of his associates, without the consent of the respondent,—

    (a) to enter upon the servient land for the purpose of carrying out the specified works;

    (b) to bring on to that land, leave there during the period permitted by the order and, before the end of that period, remove, such materials, plant and equipment as are reasonably necessary for the carrying out of those works; and

    (c) to bring on to that land any waste arising from the carrying out of those works, if it is reasonably necessary to do so in the course of removing it from the dominant land;

but nothing in this Act or in any access order shall authorise the applicant or any of his associates to leave anything in, on or over the servient land (otherwise than in discharge of their duty to make good that land) after their entry for the purpose of carrying out works to the dominant land ceases to be authorised under or by virtue of the order.

(3) An access order requires the applicant—

    (a) to secure that any waste arising from the carrying out of the specified works is removed from the servient land forthwith;

    (b) to secure that, before the entry ceases to be authorised under or by virtue of the order, the servient land is, so far as reasonably practicable, made good; and

    (c) to indemnify the respondent against any damage which may be caused to the servient land or any goods by the applicant or any of his associates which would not have been so caused had the order not been made;

but this subsection is subject to subsections (4) and (5) below.

(4) In making an access order, the court may vary or exclude, in whole or in part,—

    (a) any authorisation that would otherwise be conferred by subsection (2)(b) or (c) above; or

    (b) any requirement that would otherwise be imposed by subsection (3) above.

(5) Without prejudice to the generality of subsection (4) above, if the court is satisfied that it is reasonably necessary for any such waste as may arise from the carrying out of the specified works to be left on the servient land for some period before removal, the access order may, in place of subsection (3)(a) above, include provision—

    (a) authorising the waste to be left on that land for such period as may be permitted by the order; and (*b*) requiring the applicant to secure that the waste is removed before the end of that period.

(6) Where the applicant or any of his associates is authorised or required under or by virtue of an access order or this section to enter, or do any other thing, upon the servient land, he shall not (as respects that access order) be taken to be a trespasser from the beginning on account of his, or any other person's, subsequent conduct.

(7) For the purposes of this section, the applicant's 'associates' are such number of persons (whether or not servants or agents of his) whom he may reasonably authorise under this subsection to exercise the power of entry conferred by the access order as may be reasonably necessary for carrying out the specified works.

4   Persons bound by access order, unidentified persons and bar on contracting out

(1) In addition to the respondent, an access order shall, subject to the provisions of the Land Charges Act 1972 and the Land Registration Act 1925, be binding on—

(*a*) any of his successors in title to the servient land; and

(*b*) any person who has an estate or interest in, or right over, the whole or any part of the servient land which was created after the making of the order and who derives his title to that estate, interest or right under the respondent;

and references to the respondent shall be construed accordingly.

(2) If and to the extent that the court considers it just and equitable to allow him to do so, a person on whom an access order becomes binding by virtue of subsection (1)(*a*) or (*b*) above shall be entitled, as respects anything falling to be done after the order becomes binding on him, to enforce the order or any of its terms or conditions as if he were the respondent, and references to the respondent shall be construed accordingly.

(3) Rules of court may—

(*a*) provide a procedure which may be followed where the applicant does not know, and cannot reasonably ascertain, the name of any person whom he desires to make respondent to the application; and

(*b*) make provision enabling such an applicant to make such a person respondent by description instead of by name;

and in this subsection 'applicant' includes a person who proposes to make an application for an access order.

(4) Any agreement, whenever made, shall be void if and to the extent that it would, apart from this subsection, prevent a person from applying for an access order or restrict his right to do so.

5   Registration of access orders and of applications for such orders

(1) In section 6(1) of the Land Charges Act 1972 (which specifies the writs and orders affecting land that may be entered in the register) after paragraph (c) there shall be added—

'(d) any access order under the Access to Neighbouring Land Act 1992.'

(2) In section 49 of the Land Registration Act 1925 (rules to provide for certain rights, interests and claims to be protected by notice) in subsection (1) (which specifies those rights, interests and claims) after paragraph (h) there shall be added—

'(j) Access orders under the Access to Neighbouring Land Act 1992 which, notwithstanding section 59 of this Act, it may be deemed expedient to protect by notice instead of by caution.'

(3) In section 64 of that Act (production of certificates for noting on certain dealings etc) after subsection (6) there shall be added—

'(7) Subsection (1) above shall also not require the production of the land certificate or of any charge certificate when a person applies for the registration of a notice in respect of an access order under the Access to Neighbouring Land Act 1992.'

(4) In any case where—

(a) an access order is discharged under section 6(1)(a) below; and

(b) the order has been protected by an entry registered under the Land Charges Act 1972 or by a notice or caution under the Land Registration Act 1925,

the court may by order direct that the entry, notice or caution shall be cancelled.

(5) The rights conferred on a person by or under an access order are not capable of constituting an overriding interest within the meaning of the Land Registration Act 1925, notwithstanding that he or any other person is in actual occupation of the whole or any part of the servient land in question.

(6) An application for an access order shall be regarded as a pending land action for the purposes of the Land Charges Act 1972 and the Land Registration Act 1925.

6   Variation of orders and damages for breach

(1) Where an access order or an order under this subsection has been made, the court may, on the application of any party to the proceedings in which the order was made or of any other person on whom the order is binding—

(a) discharge or vary the order or any of its terms or conditions;

(b) suspend any of its terms or conditions; or

(c) revive any term or condition suspended under paragraph (b) above;

and in the application of subsections (1) and (2) of section 4 above in relation to an access order, any order under this subsection which relates to the access order shall be treated for the purposes of those subsections as included in the access order.

(2) If any person contravenes or fails to comply with any requirement, term or condition imposed upon him by or under this Act, the court may, without prejudice to any other remedy available, make an order for the payment of damages by him to any other person affected by the contravention or failure who makes an application for relief under this subsection.

7   Jurisdiction over, and allocation of, proceedings

(1) The High Court and the county courts shall both have jurisdiction under this Act.

(2) In article 4 of the High Court and County Courts Jurisdiction Order 1991 (which provides that proceedings in which the county courts and the High Court both have jurisdiction may, subject to articles 5 and 6, be commenced either in a county court or in the High Court) for the words 'and 6' there shall be substituted the words, '6 and 6A'; and after article 6 of that Order there shall be inserted—

'6A. Applications under section 1 of the Access to Neighbouring Land Act 1992 shall be commenced in a county court.'

(3) The amendment by subsection (2) above of provisions contained in an order shall not be taken to have prejudiced any power to make further orders revoking or amending those provisions.

8   Interpretation and application

(1) Any reference in this Act to an 'entry' upon any servient land includes a reference to the doing on that land of anything necessary for carrying out the works to the dominant land which are reasonably necessary for its preservation; and 'enter' shall be construed accordingly.

(2) This Act applies in relation to any obstruction of, or other interference with, a right over, or interest in, any land as it applies in relation to an entry upon that land; and 'enter' and 'entry' shall be construed accordingly.

(3) In this Act—

'access order' has the meaning given by section 1(1) above;

'applicant' means a person making an application for an access order and, subject to section 4 above, 'the respondent' means the respondent, or any of the respondents, to such an application;

'the court' means the High Court or a county court;

'the dominant land' and 'the servient land' respectively have the meanings given by section 1(1) above, but subject, in the case of servient land, to section 2(1) above;

'land' does not include a highway;

'the specified works' means the works specified in the access order in pursuance of section 2(1)(a) above.

9 Short title commencement and extent

(1) This Act may be cited as the Access to Neighbouring Land Act 1992.

(2) This Act shall come into force on such day as the Lord Chancellor may by order made by statutory instrument appoint.

(3) This Act extends to England and Wales only.

* * * * *

Party Wall etc Act 1996

ARRANGEMENT OF SECTIONS

Construction and repair of walls on line of junction

Adjacent excavation and construction

Rights etc

Resolution of disputes

Expenses

An Act to make provision in respect of party walls, and excavation and construction in proximity to certain buildings or structures; and for connected purposes. [18th July 1996]

Construction and repair of walls on line of junction

1   New building on line of junction

(1) This section shall have effect where lands of different owners adjoin and—

(a)   are not built on at the line of junction; or

(b)   are built on at the line of junction only to the extent of a boundary wall (not being a party fence wall or the external wall of a building),

and either owner is about to build on any part of the line of junction.

(2) If a building owner desires to build a party wall or party fence wall on the line of junction he shall, at least one month before he intends the building work to start, serve on any adjoining owner a notice which indicates his desire to build and describes the intended wall.

(3) If, having been served with notice described in subsection (2), an adjoining owner serves on the building owner a notice indicating his consent to the building of a party wall or party fence wall—

(a)   the wall shall be built half on the land of each of the two owners or in such other position as may be agreed between the two owners; and

(b)   the expense of building the wall shall be from time to time defrayed by the two owners in such proportion as has regard to the use made or to be made of the wall by each of them and to the cost of labour and materials prevailing at the time when that use is made by each owner respectively.

(4) If, having been served with notice described in subsection (2), an adjoining owner does not consent under this subsection to the building of a party wall or party fence wall, the building owner may only build the wall—

(a) at his own expense; and

(b) as an external wall or a fence wall, as the case may be, placed wholly on his own land,

and consent under this subsection is consent by a notice served within the period of fourteen days beginning with the day on which the notice described in subsection (2) is served.

(5) If the building owner desires to build on the line of junction a wall placed wholly on his own land he shall, at least one month before he intends the building work to start, serve on any adjoining owner a notice which indicates his desire to build and describes the intended wall.

(6) Where the building owner builds a wall wholly on his own land in accordance with subsection (4) or (5) he shall have the right, at any time in the period which—

(a) begins one month after the day on which the notice mentioned in the subsection concerned was served, and

(b) ends twelve months after that day,

to place below the level of the land of the adjoining owner such projecting footings and foundations as are necessary for the construction of the wall.

(7) Where the building owner builds a wall wholly on his own land in accordance with subsection (4) or (5) he shall do so at his own expense and shall compensate any adjoining owner and any adjoining occupier for any damage to his property occasioned by—

(a) the building of the wall;

(b) the placing of any footings or foundations placed in accordance with subsection (6).

(8) Where any dispute arises under this section between the building owner and any adjoining owner or occupier it is to be determined in accordance with section 10.

2 Repair etc of party wall: rights of owner

(1) This section applies where lands of different owners adjoin and at the line of junction the said lands are built on or a boundary wall, being a party fence wall or the external wall of a building, has been erected.

(2) A building owner shall have the following rights—

(a) to underpin, thicken or raise a party structure, a party fence wall, or an external wall which belongs to the building owner and is built against a party structure or party fence wall;

(b) to make good, repair, or demolish and rebuild, a party structure or party fence wall in a case where such work is necessary on account of defect or want of repair of the structure or wall;

(c) to demolish a partition which separates buildings belonging to different owners but does not conform with statutory requirements and to build instead a party wall which does so conform;

(d) in the case of buildings connected by arches or structures over public ways or over passages belonging to other persons, to demolish the whole or part of such buildings, arches or structures which do not conform with statutory requirements and to rebuild them so that they do so conform;

(e) to demolish a party structure which is of insufficient strength or height for the purposes of any intended building of the building owner and to rebuild it of sufficient strength or height for the said purposes (including rebuilding to a lesser height or thickness where the rebuilt structure is of sufficient strength and height for the purposes of any adjoining owner);

(f) to cut into a party structure for any purpose (which may be or include the purpose of inserting a damp proof course);

(g) to cut away from a party wall, party fence wall, external wall or boundary wall any footing or any projecting chimney breast, jamb or flue, or other projection on or over the land of the building owner in order to erect, raise or underpin any such wall or for any other purpose;

(h) to cut away or demolish parts of any wall or building of an adjoining owner overhanging the land of the building owner or overhanging a party wall, to the extent that it is necessary to cut away or demolish the parts to enable a vertical wall to be erected or raised against the wall or building of the adjoining owner;

(j) to cut into the wall of an adjoining owner's building in order to insert a flashing or other weather-proofing of a wall erected against that wall;

(k) to execute any other necessary works incidental to the connection of a party structure with the premises adjoining it;

(l) to raise a party fence wall, or to raise such a wall for use as a party wall, and to demolish a party fence wall and rebuild it as a party fence wall or as a party wall;

(m) subject to the provisions of section 11(7), to reduce, or to demolish and rebuild, a party wall or party fence wall to—
  (i) a height of not less than two metres where the wall is not used by an adjoining owner to any greater extent than a boundary wall; or
  (ii) a height currently enclosed upon by the building of an adjoining owner;

(n) to expose a party wall or party structure hitherto enclosed subject to providing adequate weathering.

(3) Where work mentioned in paragraph (a) of subsection (2) is not

necessary on account of defect or want of repair of the structure or wall concerned, the right falling within that paragraph is exercisable—

(a) subject to making good all damage occasioned by the work to the adjoining premises or to their internal furnishings and decorations; and

(b) where the work is to a party structure or external wall, subject to carrying any relevant flues and chimney stacks up to such a height and in such materials as may be agreed between the building owner and the adjoining owner concerned or, in the event of dispute, determined in accordance with section 10;

and relevant flues and chimney stacks are those which belong to an adjoining owner and either form part of or rest on or against the party structure or external wall.

(4) The right falling within subsection (2)(e) is exercisable subject to—

(a) making good all damage occasioned by the work to the adjoining premises or to their internal furnishings and decorations; and

(b) carrying any relevant flues and chimney stacks up to such a height and in such materials as may be agreed between the building owner and the adjoining owner concerned or, in the event of dispute, determined in accordance with section 10;

and relevant flues and chimney stacks are those which belong to an adjoining owner and either form part of or rest on or against the party structure.

(5) Any right falling within subsection (2)(f), (g) or (h) is exercisable subject to making good all damage occasioned by the work to the adjoining premises or to their internal furnishings and decorations.

(6) The right falling within subsection (2)(j) is exercisable subject to making good all damage occasioned by the work to the wall of the adjoining owner's building.

(7) The right falling within subsection (2)(m) is exercisable subject to—

(a) reconstructing any parapet or replacing an existing parapet with another one; or

(b) constructing a parapet where one is needed but did not exist before.

(8) For the purposes of this section a building or structure which was erected before the day on which this Act was passed shall be deemed to conform with statutory requirements if it conforms with the statutes regulating buildings or structures on the date on which it was erected.

3 Party structure notices

(1) Before exercising any right conferred on him by section 2 a building owner shall serve on any adjoining owner a notice (in this Act referred to as a 'party structure notice') stating—

(a) the name and address of the building owner;

(b) the nature and particulars of the proposed work including, in cases where the building owner proposes to construct special foundations, plans, sections and details of construction of the special foundations together with reasonable particulars of the loads to be carried thereby; and

(c) the date on which the proposed work will begin.

(2) A party structure notice shall—

(a) be served at least two months before the date on which the proposed work will begin;

(b) cease to have effect if the work to which it relates—
  (i) has not begun within the period of twelve months beginning with the day on which the notice is served; and
  (ii) is not prosecuted with due diligence.

(3) Nothing in this section shall—

(a) prevent a building owner from exercising with the consent in writing of the adjoining owners and of the adjoining occupiers any right conferred on him by section 2; or

(b) require a building owner to serve any party structure notice before complying with any notice served under any statutory provisions relating to dangerous or neglected structures.

4   Counter notices

(1) An adjoining owner may, having been served with a party structure notice serve on the building owner a notice (in this Act referred to as a 'counter notice') setting out—

(a) in respect of a party fence wall or party structure, a requirement that the building owner build in or on the wall or structure to which the notice relates such chimney copings, breasts, jambs or flues, or such piers or recesses or other like works, as may reasonably be required for the convenience of the adjoining owner;

(b) in respect of special foundations to which the adjoining owner consents under section 7(4) below, a requirement that the special foundations—
  (i) be placed at a specified greater depth than that proposed by the building owner; or
  (ii) be constructed of sufficient strength to bear the load to be carried by columns of any intended building of the adjoining owner,

or both.

(2) A counter notice shall—

(a) specify the works required by the notice to be executed and shall be accompanied by plans, sections and particulars of such works; and

(b) be served within the period of one month beginning with the day on which the party structure notice is served.

(3) A building owner on whom a counter notice has been served shall

comply with the requirements of the counter notice unless the execution of the works required by the counter notice would—

(a) be injurious to him;

(b) cause unnecessary inconvenience to him; or

(c) cause unnecessary delay in the execution of the works pursuant to the party structure notice.

5 Disputes arising under sections 3 and 4

If an owner on whom a party structure notice or a counter notice has been served does not serve a notice indicating his consent to it within the period of fourteen days beginning with the day on which the party structure notice or counter notice was served, he shall be deemed to have dissented from the notice and a dispute shall be deemed to have arisen between the parties.

Adjacent excavation and construction

6 Adjacent excavation and construction

(1) This section applies where—

(a) a building owner proposes to excavate, or excavate for and erect a building or structure, within a distance of three metres measured horizontally from any part of a building or structure of an adjoining owner; and

(b) any part of the proposed excavation, building or structure will within those three metres extend to a lower level than the level of the bottom of the foundations of the building or structure of the adjoining owner.

(2) This section also applies where—

(a) a building owner proposes to excavate, or excavate for and erect a building or structure, within a distance of six metres measured horizontally from any part of a building or structure of an adjoining owner; and

(b) any part of the proposed excavation, building or structure will within those six metres meet a plane drawn downwards in the direction of the excavation, building or structure of the building owner at an angle of forty-five degrees to the horizontal from the line formed by the intersection of the plane of the level of the bottom of the foundations of the building or structure of the adjoining owner with the plane of the external face of the external wall of the building or structure of the adjoining owner.

(3) The building owner may, and if required by the adjoining owner shall, at his own expense underpin or otherwise strengthen or safeguard the foundations of the building or structure of the adjoining owner so far as may be necessary.

(4) Where the buildings or structures of different owners are within the

respective distances mentioned in subsections (1) and (2) the owners of those buildings or structures shall be deemed to be adjoining owners for the purposes of this section.

(5) In any case where this section applies the building owner shall, at least one month before beginning to excavate, or excavate for and erect a building or structure, serve on the adjoining owner a notice indicating his proposals and stating whether he proposes to underpin or otherwise strengthen or safeguard the foundations of the building or structure of the adjoining owner.

(6) The notice referred to in subsection (5) shall be accompanied by plans and sections showing—

(a) the site and depth of any excavation the building owner proposes to make;

(b) if he proposes to erect a building or structure, its site.

(7) If an owner on whom a notice referred to in subsection (5) has been served does not serve a notice indicating his consent to it within the period of fourteen days beginning with the day on which the notice referred to in subsection (5) was served, he shall be deemed to have dissented from the notice and a dispute shall be deemed to have arisen between the parties.

(8) The notice referred to in subsection (5) shall cease to have effect if the work to which the notice relates—

(a) has not begun within the period of twelve months beginning with the day on which the notice was served; and

(b) is not prosecuted with due diligence.

(9) On completion of any work executed in pursuance of this section the building owner shall if so requested by the adjoining owner supply him with particulars including plans and sections of the work.

(10) Nothing in this section shall relieve the building owner from any liability to which he would otherwise be subject for injury to any adjoining owner or any adjoining occupier by reason of work executed by him.

Rights etc

7   Compensation etc

(1) A building owner shall not exercise any right conferred on him by this Act in such a manner or at such time as to cause unnecessary inconvenience to any adjoining owner or to any adjoining occupier.

(2) The building owner shall compensate any adjoining owner and any adjoining occupier for any loss or damage which may result to any of them by reason of any work executed in pursuance of this Act.

(3) Where a building owner in exercising any right conferred on him by this Act lays open any part of the adjoining land or building he shall at his own expense make and maintain so long as may be necessary a proper hoarding, shoring or fans or temporary construction for the protection of the adjoining land or building and the security of any adjoining occupier.

(4) Nothing in this Act shall authorise the building owner to place special foundations on land of an adjoining owner without his previous consent in writing.

(5) Any works executed in pursuance of this Act shall—

(a) comply with the provisions of statutory requirements; and

(b) be executed in accordance with such plans, sections and particulars as may be agreed between the owners or in the event of dispute determined in accordance with section 10;

and no deviation shall be made from those plans, sections and particulars except such as may be agreed between the owners (or surveyors acting on their behalf) or in the event of dispute determined in accordance with section 10.

8   Rights of entry

(1) A building owner, his servants, agents and workmen may during usual working hours enter and remain on any land or premises for the purpose of executing any work in pursuance of this Act and may remove any furniture or fittings or take any other action necessary for that purpose.

(2) If the premises are closed, the building owner, his agents and workmen may, if accompanied by a constable or other police officer, break open any fences or doors in order to enter the premises.

(3) No land or premises may be entered by any person under subsection (1) unless the building owner serves on the owner and the occupier of the land or premises—

(a) in case of emergency, such notice of the intention to enter as may be reasonably practicable;

(b) in any other case, such notice of the intention to enter as complies with subsection (4).

(4) Notice complies with this subsection if it is served in a period of not less than fourteen days ending with the day of the proposed entry.

(5) A surveyor appointed or selected under section 10 may during usual working hours enter and remain on any land or premises for the purpose of carrying out the object for which he is appointed or selected.

(6) No land or premises may be entered by a surveyor under subsection (5) unless the building owner who is a party to the dispute concerned serves on the owner and the occupier of the land or premises—

(a) in case of emergency, such notice of the intention to enter as may be reasonably practicable;

(b) in any other case, such notice of the intention to enter as complies with subsection (4).

9   Easements

Nothing in this Act shall—

(a) authorise any interference with an easement of light or other easements in or relating to a party wall; or (*b*) prejudicially affect any right of any person to preserve or restore any right or other thing in or connected with a party wall in case of the party wall being pulled down or rebuilt.

Resolution of disputes

10   Resolution of disputes
(1) Where a dispute arises or is deemed to have arisen between a building owner and an adjoining owner in respect of any matter connected with any work to which this Act relates either—

(*a*) both parties shall concur in the appointment of one surveyor (in this section referred to as an 'agreed surveyor'); or

(*b*) each party shall appoint a surveyor and the two surveyors so appointed shall forthwith select a third surveyor (all of whom are in this section referred to as 'the three surveyors').

(2) All appointments and selections made under this section shall be in writing and shall not be rescinded by either party.

(3) If an agreed surveyor—

(*a*) refuses to act;

(*b*) neglects to act for a period of ten days beginning with the day on which either party serves a request on him;

(*c*) dies before the dispute is settled; or

(*d*) becomes or deems himself incapable of acting,

the proceedings for settling such dispute shall begin *de novo*.

(4) If either party to the dispute—

(*a*) refuses to appoint a surveyor under subsection (1)(*b*), or

(*b*) neglects to appoint a surveyor under subsection (1)(*b*) for a period of ten days beginning with the day on which the other party serves a request on him,

the other party may make the appointment on his behalf.

(5) If, before the dispute is settled, a surveyor appointed under paragraph (*b*) of subsection (1) by a party to the dispute dies, or becomes or deems himself incapable of acting, the party who appointed him may appoint another surveyor in his place with the same power and authority.

(6) If a surveyor—

(*a*) appointed under paragraph (*b*) of subsection (1) by a party to the dispute; or

(*b*) appointed under subsection (4) or (5),

refuses to act effectively, the surveyor of the other party may proceed to act *ex parte* and anything so done by him shall be as effectual as if he had been an agreed surveyor.

(7) If a surveyor—

(*a*) appointed under paragraph (*b*) of subsection (1) by a party to the dispute; or

(*b*) appointed under subsection (4) or (5),

neglects to act effectively for a period of ten days beginning with the day on which either party or the surveyor of the other party serves a request on him, the surveyor of the other party may proceed to act *ex parte* in respect of the subject matter of the request and anything so done by him shall be as effectual as if he had been an agreed surveyor.

(8) If either surveyor appointed under subsection (1)(*b*) by a party to the dispute refuses to select a third surveyor under subsection (1) or (9), or neglects to do so for a period of ten days beginning with the day on which the other surveyor serves a request on him—

(*a*) the appointing officer; or

(*b*) in cases where the relevant appointing officer or his employer is a party to the dispute, the Secretary of State,

may on the application of either surveyor select a third surveyor who shall have the same power and authority as if he had been selected under subsection (1) or subsection (9).

(9) If a third surveyor selected under subsection (1)(*b*)—

(*a*) refuses to act;

(*b*) neglects to act for a period of ten days beginning with the day on which either party or the surveyor appointed by either party serves a request on him; or

(*c*) dies, or becomes or deems himself incapable of acting, before the dispute is settled,

the other two of the three surveyors shall forthwith select another surveyor in his place with the same power and authority.

(10) The agreed surveyor or as the case may be the three surveyors or any two of them shall settle by award any matter—

(*a*) which is connected with any work to which this Act relates, and

(*b*) which is in dispute between the building owner and the adjoining owner.

(11) Either of the parties or either of the surveyors appointed by the parties may call upon the third surveyor selected in pursuance of this section to determine the disputed matters and he shall make the necessary award.

(12) An award may determine—

(*a*) the right to execute any work;

(*b*) the time and manner of executing any work; and

(*c*) any other matter arising out of or incidental to the dispute including the costs of making the award;

but any period appointed by the award for executing any work shall not unless otherwise agreed between the building owner and the adjoining owner begin to run until after the expiration of the period prescribed by this Act for service of the notice in respect of which the dispute arises or is deemed to have arisen.

(13) The reasonable costs incurred in—

(*a*) making or obtaining an award under this section;

(*b*) reasonable inspections of work to which the award relates; and

(c) any other matter arising out of the dispute,
shall be paid by such of the parties as the surveyor or surveyors making the
award determine.

(14) Where the surveyors appointed by the parties make an award the
surveyors shall serve it forthwith on the parties.

(15) Where an award is made by the third surveyor—

(a) he shall, after payment of the costs of the award, serve it forthwith
on the parties or their appointed surveyors; and

(b) if it is served on their appointed surveyors, they shall serve it
forthwith on the parties.

(16) The award shall be conclusive and shall not except as provided by
this section be questioned in any court.

(17) Either of the parties to the dispute may, within the period of
fourteen days beginning with the day on which an award made under this
section is served on him appeal to the county court against the award and
the county court may—

(a) rescind the award or modify it in such manner as the court thinks
fit; and

(b) make such order as to costs as the court thinks fit.

Expenses

11 Expenses

(1) Except as provided under this section expenses of work under this
Act shall be defrayed by the building owner.

(2) Any dispute as to responsibility for expenses shall be settled as
provided in section 10.

(3) An expense mentioned in section 1(3)(b) shall be defrayed as there
mentioned.

(4) Where work is carried out in exercise of the right mentioned in
section 2(2)(a), and the work is necessary on account of defect or want of
repair of the structure or wall concerned, the expenses shall be defrayed by
the building owner and the adjoining owner in such proportion as has
regard to—

(a) the use which the owners respectively make or may make of the
structure or wall concerned; and

(b) responsibility for the defect or want of repair concerned, if more
than one owner makes use of the structure or wall concerned.

(5) Where work is carried out in exercise of the right mentioned in
section 2(2)(b) the expenses shall be defrayed by the building owner and
the adjoining owner in such proportion as has regard to—

(a) the use which the owners respectively make or may make of the
structure or wall concerned; and

(b) responsibility for the defect or want of repair concerned, if more
than one owner makes use of the structure or wall concerned.

(6) Where the adjoining premises are laid open in exercise of the right mentioned in section 2(2)(*e*) a fair allowance in respect of disturbance and inconvenience shall be paid by the building owner to the adjoining owner or occupier.

(7) Where a building owner proposes to reduce the height of a party wall or party fence wall under section 2(2)(*m*) the adjoining owner may serve a counter notice under section 4 requiring the building owner to maintain the existing height of the wall, and in such case the adjoining owner shall pay to the building owner a due proportion of the cost of the wall so far as it exceeds—

  (*a*) two metres in height; or
  (*b*) the height currently enclosed upon by the building of the adjoining owner.

(8) Where the building owner is required to make good damage under this Act the adjoining owner has a right to require that the expenses of such making good be determined in accordance with section 10 and paid to him in lieu of the carrying out of work to make the damage good.

(9) Where—

  (*a*) works are carried out, and
  (*b*) some of the works are carried out at the request of the adjoining owner or in pursuance of a requirement made by him,

he shall defray the expenses of carrying out the works requested or required by him.

(10) Where—

  (*a*) consent in writing has been given to the construction of special foundations on land of an adjoining owner; and
  (*b*) the adjoining owner erects any building or structure and its cost is found to be increased by reason of the existence of the said foundations,

the owner of the building to which the said foundations belong shall, on receiving an account with any necessary invoices and other supporting documents within the period of two months beginning with the day of the completion of the work by the adjoining owner, repay to the adjoining owner so much of the cost as is due to the existence of the said foundations.

(11) Where use is subsequently made by the adjoining owner of work carried out solely at the expense of the building owner the adjoining owner shall pay a due proportion of the expenses incurred by the building owner in carrying out that work; and for this purpose he shall be taken to have incurred expenses calculated by reference to what the cost of the work would be if it were carried out at the time when that subsequent use is made.

12 Security for expenses

(1) An adjoining owner may serve a notice requiring the building owner before he begins any work in the exercise of the rights conferred by this Act

to give such security as may be agreed between the owners or in the event of dispute determined in accordance with section 10.

(2) Where—

(*a*) in the exercise of the rights conferred by this Act an adjoining owner requires the building owner to carry out any work the expenses of which are to be defrayed in whole or in part by the adjoining owner; or

(*b*) an adjoining owner serves a notice on the building owner under subsection (1),

the building owner may before beginning the work to which the requirement or notice relates serve a notice on the adjoining owner requiring him to give such security as may be agreed between the owners or in the event of dispute determined in accordance with section 10.

(3) If within the period of one month beginning with—

(*a*) the day on which a notice is served under subsection (2); or

(*b*) in the event of dispute, the date of the determination by the surveyor or surveyors,

the adjoining owner does not comply with the notice or the determination, the requirement or notice by him to which the building owner's notice under that subsection relates shall cease to have effect.

13 Account for work carried out

(1) Within the period of two months beginning with the day of the completion of any work executed by a building owner of which the expenses are to be wholly or partially defrayed by an adjoining owner in accordance with section 11 the building owner shall serve on the adjoining owner an account in writing showing—

(*a*) particulars and expenses of the work; and

(*b*) any deductions to which the adjoining owner or any other person is entitled in respect of old materials or otherwise;

and in preparing the account the work shall be estimated and valued at fair average rates and prices according to the nature of the work, the locality and the cost of labour and materials prevailing at the time when the work is executed.

(2) Within the period of one month beginning with the day of service of the said account the adjoining owner may serve on the building owner a notice stating any objection he may have thereto and thereupon a dispute shall be deemed to have arisen between the parties.

(3) If within that period of one month the adjoining owner does not serve notice under subsection (2) he shall be deemed to have no objection to the account.

14 Settlement of account

(1) All expenses to be defrayed by an adjoining owner in accordance with an account served under section 13 shall be paid by the adjoining owner.

(2) Until an adjoining owner pays to the building owner such expenses as aforesaid the property in any works executed under this Act to which the expenses relate shall be vested solely in the building owner.

Miscellaneous

15 Service of notices etc

(1) A notice or other document required or authorised to be served under this Act may be served on a person—

(*a*) by delivering it to him in person;

(*b*) by sending it by post to him at his usual or last-known residence or place of business in the United Kingdom; or

(*c*) in the case of a body corporate, by delivering it to the secretary or clerk of the body corporate at its registered or principal office or sending it by post to the secretary or clerk of that body corporate at that office.

(2) In the case of a notice or other document required or authorised to be served under this Act on a person as owner of premises, it may alternatively be served by—

(*a*) addressing it 'the owner' of the premises (naming them), and

(*b*) delivering it to a person on the premises or, if no person to whom it can be delivered is found there, fixing it to a conspicuous part of the premises.

16 Offences

(1) If—

(*a*) an occupier of land or premises refuses to permit a person to do anything which he is entitled to do with regard to the land or premises under section 8(1) or (5); and

(*b*) the occupier knows or has reasonable cause to believe that the person is so entitled,

the occupier is guilty of an offence.

(2) If—

(*a*) a person hinders or obstructs a person in attempting to do anything which he is entitled to do with regard to land or premises under section 8(1) or (5); and

(*b*) the first-mentioned person knows or has reasonable cause to believe that the other person is so entitled,

the first-mentioned person is guilty of an offence.

(3) A person guilty of an offence under subsection (1) or (2) is liable on summary conviction to a fine of an amount not exceeding level 3 on the standard scale.

17 Recovery of sums

Any sum payable in pursuance of this Act (otherwise than by way of fine) shall be recoverable summarily as a civil debt.

18   Exception in case of Temples etc

(1) This Act shall not apply to land which is situated in inner London and in which there is an interest belonging to—

(*a*)   the Honourable Society of the Inner Temple,

(*b*)   the Honourable Society of the Middle Temple,

(*c*)   the Honourable Society of Lincoln's Inn, or

(*d*)   the Honourable Society of Gray's Inn.

(2) The reference in subsection (1) to inner London is to Greater London other than the outer London boroughs.

19   The Crown

(1) This Act shall apply to land in which there is—

(*a*)   an interest belonging to Her Majesty in right of the Crown,

(*b*)   an interest belonging to a government department, or

(*c*)   an interest held in trust for Her Majesty for the purposes of any such department.

(2) This Act shall apply to—

(*a*)   land which is vested in, but not occupied by, Her Majesty in right of the Duchy of Lancaster;

(*b*)   land which is vested in, but not occupied by, the possessor for the time being of the Duchy of Cornwall.

20   Interpretation

In this Act, unless the context otherwise requires, the following expressions have the meanings hereby respectively assigned to them—

'adjoining owner' and 'adjoining occupier' respectively mean any owner and any occupier of land, buildings, storeys or rooms adjoining those of the building owner and for the purposes only of section 6 within the distances specified in that section;

'appointing officer' means the person appointed under this Act by the local authority to make such appointments as are required under section 10(8);

'building owner' means an owner of land who is desirous of exercising rights under this Act;

'foundation', in relation to a wall, means the solid ground or artificially formed support resting on solid ground on which the wall rests;

'owner' includes—

(*a*)   a person in receipt of, or entitled to receive, the whole or part of the rents or profits of land;

(*b*)   a person in possession of land, otherwise than as a mortgagee or as a tenant from year to year or for a lesser term or as a tenant at will;

(*c*)   a purchaser of an interest in land under a contract for purchase or under an agreement for a lease, otherwise than under an agreement for a tenancy from year to year or for a lesser term;

'party fence wall' means a wall (not being part of a building) which stands on lands of different owners and is used or constructed to be used for separating such adjoining lands, but does not include a wall constructed on the land of one owner the artificially formed support of which projects into the land of another owner;

'party structure' means a party wall and also a floor partition or other structure separating buildings or parts of buildings approached solely by separate staircases or separate entrances;

'party wall' means—

(a) a wall which forms part of a building and stands on lands of different owners to a greater extent than the projection of any artificially formed support on which the wall rests; and

(b) so much of a wall not being a wall referred to in paragraph (a) above as separates buildings belonging to different owners;

'special foundations' means foundations in which an assemblage of beams or rods is employed for the purpose of distributing any load; and

'surveyor' means any person not being a party to the matter appointed or selected under section 10 to determine disputes in accordance with the procedures set out in this Act.

21 Other statutory provisions

(1) The Secretary of State may by order amend or repeal any provision of a private or local Act passed before or in the same session as this Act, if it appears to him necessary or expedient to do so in consequence of this Act.

(2) An order under subsection (1) may—

(a) contain such savings or transitional provisions as the Secretary of State thinks fit;

(b) make different provision for different purposes.

(3) The power to make an order under subsection (1) shall be exercisable by statutory instrument subject to annulment in pursuance of a resolution of either House of Parliament.

General

22 Short title, commencement and extent

(1) This Act may be cited as the Party Wall etc Act 1996.

(2) This Act shall come into force in accordance with provision made by the Secretary of State by order made by statutory instrument.

(3) An order under subsection (2) may—

(a) contain such savings or transitional provisions as the Secretary of State thinks fit;

(b) make different provision for different purposes.

(4) This Act extends to England and Wales only.

Appendix 2

Statutory Instruments

Land Registration Rules 1925

276 Fixed boundaries

If it is desired to indicate on the filed plan or General Map, or otherwise to define in the register, the precise position of the boundaries of the land or any parts thereof, notice shall be given to the owners and occupiers of the adjoining lands, in each instance, of the intention to ascertain and fix the boundary, with such plan, or tracing, or extract from the proposed verbal description of the land as may be necessary, to show clearly the fixed boundary proposed to be registered; and any question of doubt or dispute arising therefrom shall be dealt with as provided by these rules.

277 Note as to fixed boundaries in register

When the position and description of the boundaries of the land have been thus ascertained and determined, the necessary particulars shall be added to the filed plan or General Map, and a note shall be made in the Property Register to the effect that the boundaries have been fixed. The plan or General Map shall then be deemed to define accurately the fixed boundaries.

278 General boundaries

(1) Except in cases in which it is noted in the Property Register that the boundaries have been fixed, the filed plan or General Map shall be deemed to indicate the general boundaries only.

(2) In such cases the exact line of the boundary will be left undetermined—as, for instance, whether it includes a hedge or wall and ditch, or runs along the centre of a wall or fence, or its inner or outer face, or how far it runs within or beyond it; or whether or not the land registered includes the whole or any portion of an adjoining road or stream.

(3) When a general boundary only is desired to be entered in the register, notice to the owners of the adjoining lands need not be given.

(4) This rule shall apply notwithstanding that a part or the whole of a ditch, wall, fence, road, stream, or other boundary is expressly included in or excluded from the title or that it forms the whole of the land comprised in the title.

* * * * *

County Court Rules 1981

ORDER 49
MISCELLANEOUS STATUTES

1 Access to Neighbouring Land Act 1992

(1) In this rule, 'the 1992 Act' means the Access to Neighbouring Land Act 1992, a section referred to by a number means the section so numbered in the 1992 Act and expressions which are defined in the 1992 Act have the same meaning in this rule as they have in that Act.

(2) An application for an access order under section 1 of the 1992 Act shall be made by originating application which shall be filed in the court for the district in which the dominant land is situated.

(3) The application shall—

(a) identify the dominant land and the servient land and state whether the dominant land is or includes residential land;

(b) specify the works alleged to be necessary for the preservation of the whole or a part of the dominant land;

(c) state why entry upon the servient land is required and specify the area to which access is required by reference, if possible, to a plan annexed to the application;

(d) give the name of the person who will be carrying out the works if it is known at the time of the application;

(e) state the proposed date on which, or the dates between which, the works are to be started and their approximate duration; and

(f) state what (if any) provision has been made by way of insurance in the event of possible injury to persons or damage to property arising out of the proposed works.

(4) The respondents shall be the owner and the occupier of the servient land and any respondent who wishes to be heard on the application shall file an answer within 14 days after the date of service of the application on him.

(5) Order 24, rule 3 shall apply with the necessary modifications to service of the originating application under this rule.

(6) The court may direct that notice of the application shall be given to any person who may be affected by the proposed entry and any such person may, within 14 days after service of the notice on him, apply to be made a respondent to the application.

(7) The application may be heard and determined by the district judge and may, if the court thinks fit, be dealt with in chambers.

Town & Country Planning (General Permitted Development) Order 1995

3 Permitted development

(1) Subject to the provisions of this Order and regulations 60 to 63 of the Conservation (Natural Habitats, &c.) Regulations 1994(*a*) (general development orders), planning permission is hereby granted for the classes of development described as permitted development in Schedule 2.

(2) Any permission granted by paragraph (1) is subject to any relevant exception, limitation or condition specified in Schedule 2.

SCHEDULE 2
PART 2
MINOR OPERATIONS

A The erection, construction, maintenance, improvement or alteration of a gate, fence, wall or other means of enclosure

A1 Development is not permitted by Class A if—

(*a*) the height of any gate, fence, wall or means of enclosure erected or constructed adjacent to a highway used by vehicular traffic would, after the carrying out of the development, exceed one metre above ground level;

(*b*) the height of any other gate, fence, wall or means of enclosure erected or constructed would exceed two metres above ground level;

(*c*) the height of any gate, fence, wall or other means of enclosure maintained, improved or altered would, as a result of the development, exceed its former height or the height referred to in sub-paragraph (*a*) or (*b*) as the height appropriate to it if erected or constructed, whichever is the greater; or

(*d*) it would involve development within the curtilage of, or to a gate, fence, wall or other means of enclosure surrounding, a listed building.

Index